AF522234

FOOD TOURISM

By

Alek Clark

DISCOVERY PUBLISHING HOUSE PVT. LTD.
NEW DELHI-110 002

Published by:
Namit Wasan
DISCOVERY PUBLISHING HOUSE PVT. LTD.
4383/4B, Ansari Road, Darya Ganj
New Delhi-110 002 (India)
Phone : +91-11-23279245; 23253475; 43596065
E-mail : discoverybooksindia@gmail.com
discoverypublishinghouse@gmail.com
namitwasan9@gmail.com
web : www.discoverypublishinggroup.com

Reprinted: **2019**

First Edition: **2011**

ISBN: 978-81-8356-895-1

Food Tourism

Printed at:
Infinity Imaging Systems
Delhi

Preface

Good food and fine wines are a vital part of any travel experience. In recent years, they are increasingly being seen as prime travel motivators in their own right, which has led to rapid growth in the food tourism niche.

The increase in culinary travel goes along with a rise in emphasis on food throughout the American and European cultures. Today's typical tourist is much more educated than his predecessors 20 years ago, he is constantly searching for new experiences and adventures, is interested in leading a healthy lifestyle and wants to experience the local culture when he goes on holiday.

Extra-ordinary restaurant experiences, wine tasting and cooking classes have always played an important role in traditional gastro destinations like France, Italy and California . More and more specialised operators offer food and wine holidays in these countries, and also in various emerging food tourism markets like Australia, Chile, Mexico, Turkey, Croatia, Austria and Switzerland.

France has long been a tourist destination, and not without compelling reasons. A great traditional background, great food, and great wines! Tourists in France can visit the many vineyards in France and watch how wines are made. Trust us, next time, the same wine will taste better! They can also sample a number of different types and years of wines that were made at the vineyard. They can often even travel around the vineyard and pick grapes right off the stem.

According to research by the Future Foundation families are also becoming increasingly democratic in food choice, as children get older they have more influence in what they eat and where the family eats. Children are also spending increasing amounts of time with their grandparents with over two-thirds of children born between 1978 and 1986 being looked after by their grandparents at least once a month, compared to one quarter of those born in 1937 or earlier.

Contents

CHAPTER-1

Food Tourism : An Innovative Concept

It could be the colorful sight of a giant rustic paella in a Spanish seaside town or the smell of a warm bagel on a New York street. But whatever the dish, it seems food is something an increasing number of us remember from our travels. Like never before, holiday makers are choosing where they go by what they can put in their stomachs and catering for them is now top of the menu for tour operators and destinations.

Fiona Jeffery, Group Exhibition Director of World Travel Market, who undertook the independent research with 2000 people throughout the UK of all ages and socio economic groups, said: "Food tourism today is where eco-tourism was 20 years ago; people are starting to take an interest.

"Although the research was carried out on behalf of World Travel Market was in the UK, we believe it is representative of a new and growing phenomenon within the international industry.

Good food and fine wines are a vital part of any travel experience. In recent years, they are increasingly being seen as prime travel motivators in their own right, which has led to rapid growth in the food tourism niche.

The increase in culinary travel goes along with a rise in emphasis on food throughout the American and European cultures. Today's typical tourist is much more educated than his predecessors 20 years ago, he is constantly searching for new experiences and adventures, is interested in leading a healthy lifestyle and wants to experience the local culture when he goes on holiday.

Extra-ordinary restaurant experiences, wine tasting and cooking classes have always played an important role in traditional gastro destinations like France, Italy and California . More and more specialised operators offer food and wine holidays in these countries, and also in various emerging food tourism markets like Australia, Chile, Mexico, Turkey, Croatia, Austria and Switzerland.

Most of these tours are guided; but some operators offer self-drive versions, too. The guided tours typically include wine tasting, lunches and dinners in special locations, demonstrations by chef cooks, visiting local markets and sightseeing. Special tours offer hiking or biking in wine regions, a visit to European Christmas Markets and various other experiences related to cooking and eating.

The distinguished traveller might rather choose a custom food and wine tour instead, making his own choices about where to stay, to eat and to drink. Even if you don't intend to use a specialised food travel operator you'll find countless options for making food and wine an important part of your next vacation.

After all, there's not much that beats an evening at a wonderful holiday location, eating mouth-watering delicatessen and drinking a fine glass of wine. Hopefully we have managed to whet your appetite for food travel.

Wine is not a very complex drink, considering the basic idea of wine. It is made from grapes that have been turned into juice. The juice is allowed to ferment and the result is wine. That's it! But, it is this fermentation process that is critical in wine-making, this itself decides most palate properties of the wine. Not that the quality of grapes is irrelevant, though. There are a number of different varieties and types of wine, beginning with the basic white and red. People around the world are beginning to love wine. They are enjoying it, in fact, so much that many are touring the world just to taste brands specific to some parts of the world.

The finest of India's cuisines is as rich and diverse as it's civilization. It is an art form that has been passed on through generations purely by word of mouth, from guru teacher) to vidhyarthi (pupil) or from mother to daughter.

The hospitality of the Indians is legendary. In Sanskrit literature the three famous words 'Atithi Devo Bhava' or 'The guest is truly your god' are a dictum of hospitality in India. Indians believe that they are honoured if they share their mealtimes with guests. Even the poorest look forward to guests and are willing to share this meager food with guest.

A wine tour is when a traveler goes to specific destinations in order to view wine being made or taste a variety of different wines. Some are lucky enough to have vineyards a short distance away, but others need to travel thousands of miles in order to taste that elusive glass of wine that they have been searching for. Not that they would mind!

The difference in wines comes in the fermenting process and in the grapes. There are dozens of types of grapes, and each grape ferments a little differently than any other. When more than two grapes are added together, another type of wine is formed. This means that there are dozens of different subtle nuances in the smell, look, and flavor of the wine.

WINE CULTURE

It used to be that people only drank wine when they were out at a fancy restaurant. Now, however, wine is widely available, even at places you may not normally expect - try your neighborhood grocery store for some inexpensive flavor! There are inexpensive wines, including some that come in boxes, and there are expensive wines, which are more elaborately decorated and packaged. Most agree that it is not necessarily the cost that matters when it comes to the taste, but that more expensive wines often taste a bit more refined. Some people even try to collect wines that they enjoy, especially wines that considered to be vintage.

France

France has long been a tourist destination, and not without compelling reasons. A great traditional background, great food, and great wines! Tourists in France can visit the many vineyards in France and watch how wines are made. Trust us, next time, the same wine will taste better! They can also sample a number of different types and years of wines that were made at the vineyard. They can often even travel around the vineyard and pick grapes right off the stem.

Anybody that enjoys wine would enjoy a trip that is revolves around wine tourism. This is not to say that the tourist can not enjoy the other sites as well, but when wine is the center of the trip, the tourist is sure to have a good time. Enjoy your drinking, but remember, don't drive after that!

Culinary tourism or food tourism is experiencing the food of the country, region or area, and is now considered a vital component of the tourism experience. Dining out is common among tourists and "food is believed to rank alongside climate, accommodation, and scenery" in importance to tourists.

Culinary tourism is defined as the pursuit of unique and memorable eating and drinking experiences. Culinary tourism differs from agritourism in that culinary tourism is considered a subset of cultural tourism (cuisine is a manifestation of culture) whereas agritourism is considered a subset of rural tourism, but culinary tourism and agritourism are inextricably linked, as the seeds of cuisine can be found in agriculture.

Culinary tourism is not limited to gourmet food. This is perhaps best illustrated by the notion that culinary tourism is about what is "unique and memorable, not what is necessarily pretentious and exclusive". Similarly, wine tourism and beer tourism are also regarded as subsets of culinary tourism.

ORGANIZATIONS

The International Culinary Tourism Association (ICTA) is considered the world's leading authority on culinary travel with resources and information for food, beverage and tourism industry professionals around the world. The ICTA has four main organizations:

- International Culinary Tourism Association (ICTA)
- Non-profit trade association, founded in 2003, that works as a resource center for the media and offers benefits to the members.
- International Culinary Tourism Institute (ICTI), founded in 2006, is a non-profit education organization for training and education for its members and the public.
- International Culinary Tourism Development: consulting, research, strategy and product development solutions to businesses of all culinary tourism businesses.
- FoodTrekker Publishing delivers promotional assistance and help to culinary tourism businesses.

LASSI - PUNJAB

Lassi, by far, is the most easiest Indian dish to prepare and is taken cold. It is a good way to beat the scorching heat and get refreshed.

It can prepared in two ways either sweet or salty.

SWEET LASSI

Ingredients

1 cup of yogurt

½ a cup of water

½ a cup of ice cubes

3 to 5 teaspoons of sugar

A pinch of salt

A dollop of plain yogurt for garnishing

Salty Lassi

Ingredients

Cumin seeds - 1 tsp

Plain yogurt - 1 cup

Chilled milk - 1 cup

Lemon juice - 2 tsp

Salt - 1/2 to 1 tsp

Ice cubes - 1/2 cup

A dollop of plain yogurt for garnishing

Common Preparation

1. Blend all the ingredients at high speed till frothy.
2. Add a dollop of fresh yogurt on top.
3. Make 2-3 glasses of Lassi.

Tidbit: Since usually punjabis (people who are from the Indian state of punjab) tend make huge gallons of lassi for their daily consumption, they use washing machine to churn curd/yogurt and blend the ingredients!!!

BIRYANI - HYDERABAD

Hyderabadi Biryani is a famous meat and rice dish of Hyderabad, India.

It is a traditional celebration meal made using goat meat and rice and is the staple of a die-hard Hyderabadi. The blending of mughlai and Telangana cuisines in the kitchens of the Nizam (ruler of the historic Hyderabad State), resulted in the creation of Hyderabadi Biryani.

Ingredients

1 kg: Meat

750 gm: Semi cooked rice

Sautéed brown onions to taste

1 tbsp: Ginger garlic paste

1 tbsp: Red chilli paste

1 tbsp: Green chilli paste
tbsp: Cardamom powder
3-4 sticks:
Cinnamon
1 tbsp: Cumin seeds
4-5: Cloves
2 tbsp: Lemon juice
250 gm: Curd
4 tbsp: Butter
A pinch: Mace
Mint leaves to taste
1 tsp: Saffron
½ cup: Water
1 tbsp: Salt
½ cup: Oil

Method

1. Clean the meat.
2. Now in a pan add meat, salt, ginger garlic paste, red chilli powder, green chilli paste, sautéed brown onions, cardamom powder, cinnamon, cumin seeds, cloves, mace, mint leaves and lemon juice. Mix it well.
3. Add curd, clarified butter, semi cooked rice, saffron, water and oil and mix it well.
4. Now apply sticky dough on the sides of the pan.
5. Cover with lid to seal it and cook for about 25 minutes.
6. Hyderabadi Biryani is ready to eat.
7. Garnish with boiled eggs, sliced carrot and cucumber.
8. Serve hot.

HALWA - TIRUNELVELI

This sweet (pronounced locally as ulva) is made from wheat and sugar. Halwa is brown and semi-solid in texture and contains lots of ghee/Vanaspati which gives it the oily look. It tastes the best when fresh and hot. Tirunelveli Halwa is said to owe its peculiar taste due to the recipe of this region.

Two of the famous halwa stores are Irutu Kadai halwa (Dark Store halwa), situated near the Nellayappar temple and Shanthi Sweets. The name Irutu Kadai of the former store derives from the fact that the looks of the store had been kept unchanged from the date it was started. Till date, there is no bright electrical lamp or even a board display to show the shop name!

Ingredients

Whole Wheat - 11/2 cups

Sugar - 6 cups

Ghee/Clarified Butter - 3 cups

Cashew Nuts - 15

Kesari powder - 1/4 tsp.

Method

1. Soak the raw wheat into water overnight.
2. Grind the soaked wheat in a blender or a wet grinder and extract the first milk and the second from the ground mixture.
3. Heat a thick bottomed kadai.
4. Pour both the milks into the kadai. Let the milk cook and thicken.
5. The mixture in the kadai should start looking translucent.
6. Once it becomes completely translucent start adding the sugar to the kadai. Also add the kesari powder to kadai. This gives the halwa an orange color.
7. After about 10 mins start adding the ghee slowly into the kadai. After adding all the ghee let the mixture cook until the ghee begins to separate.
8. Fry the nuts in ghee till golden brown and add it to the kadai. Switch off the gas and pour the halwa on a big plate.

9. Rub some ghee into the plate before pouring the mixture into it. Let the halwa cool for some time.
10. After it cools and thickens cut the halwa into squares and serve.

Note: The milk from the wheat can be extracted by passing the ground wheat through a minute sieve or through muslin cloth. After extracting the first milk add more water to the residual pulp and let it sit for some time. Pass this again through the sieve to get the second milk. The first milk is always thicker than the second milk.

Today's tourist is more cultured than visitors of 20 years ago, is well travelled, is searching for new experiences, is concerned about the environment, is interested in taking part in a health/well-being lifestyle and wants to experience the local culture when he goes on holiday. Trend analyst, Ian Yeoman writes that food is a significant aspect of the tourist's experience of a destination, driven by the growing trends of authenticity and the need to have a high-quality experience. Food tourism shapes gastro destinations such as France, Italy and California whereas in emerging destinations such as Croatia, Vietnam and Mexico food plays an important part of the overall experience.

NEW TRENDS IN FOOD TOURISM

Disposable Income and Spending Patterns

All across world, growing affluence of the populations has a profound impact on consumer spending. Consumers spend a higher proportion of their income on prepared food, gourmet products, eating out and food items with some form of health or ethical benefits. The key point is that according to Michael Silverstein writing in his book Trading Up: The New American Luxury the consumer has traded up where the product is aspiration or traded down when the product is only function. This is one reason why producers and retailers have focused on quality through products such as Tesco's finest range or ethical consumption, where the consumer will pay a premium for 'fair trade' product.

Demographics and Household Change

According to research by the Future Foundation families are also becoming increasingly democratic in food choice, as children get older they have more influence in what they eat and where the family eats. Children are also spending increasing amounts of time with their grandparents with over two-thirds of children born between 1978 and 1986 being looked after by their grandparents at least once a month, compared to one quarter of those born in 1937 or earlier. This increase indicates a demand for venues offering facilities that appeal to differing age groups and generations. By 2015, those aged between 45 and 59 will be part of the most populous age group in the United Kingdom. Households headed by those aged 50 plus will account for around 50% of all households, and this same age group will account for over 39% of all consumers spending on leisure goods and services. In 2004, the 50-64 age groups spent US $24.80 per household per week on restaurant meals, US $2.40 more than the national average - this will be a key market in the future. Another consequence of longevity is 'lifestyle fragmentation', the idea that life is increasingly being experienced as a series of non-linear events with no set pattern. As characteristics of different age groups becomes blurred and diverse, more people will expect the places they visit to be adaptable to different aspects of their daily lives. In other words, eating out opportunities suitable for whatever the situations requires - whether this is work, with children or simply eating alone. And finally, rising divorce rates are also good for food tourism, as Michael Silverstein observe that divorcees have to search for new partners and subsequently will take prospective partners out for dinner and away for romantic weekends.

Individualism

Individualism means uniqueness as tourists search out local, fresh and good quality cuisine that reflects the authenticity of the destination. The end of mass customisation has seen Starbucks fail in Australia as the brand is perceived as bland and lacking individuality. Gone are the days of the British tourist wanting 'egg and chips' in Ibiza or American's only eating Kentucky Fried Chicken when in Australia.

The Multi-Cultured Consumer

The whole process of globalisation has significantly amplified the meaning of the term multi-culturalism within our social order. Access to an even wider range of ideas and interests has never been easier. The Internet boom, the expansion in specialist and minority TV channels, the relentless growth in international tourism, etc., combine to stretch perceptions and eliminate that what we might call mono-culturalism; seeing the world through only one set of pre-ordained, inherited notions. The consumer of today will watch the latest Bollywood film, consume a curry, purchase exotic spices for cooking and will read about Rajasthan in the latest edition of the Lonely Planet. Multiculturalism has now become an everyday concept in the daily life of the consumer; today curry is the United Kingdom's favourite dish.

The Role of the Celebrity Chef and Media

The media has substantial influence in determining food product selection. The influence of celebrity chefs is often referred to as the 'the Delia effect' after the media chef Delia Smith, whose 1998 television programme 'How to Cook' resulted in an extra 1.3 million eggs being sold in Britain each day of the series. The phenomena of Gordon Ramsey with 'Hells Kitchen' and the 'F word' or Jamie Oliver campaign for good wholesome school dinners all drives our interest in good quality real food. The emergence of the niche food programmes, TV channels and magazines means the food celebrity and expert has been created. Today, that celebrity chef shapes tourism products, whether it is a cookery course with Rick Stein in Padstow or Martin Yan's food cruises across China.

Trend 6:

Around 30% of adults say that they have been eating less fat and sugar compared to the previous year and 28% say they are eating less salt, whereas other food groups, notably vegetables, fruit and bread/cereal/pasta/potatoes are on the rise. These trends have transformed themselves into the food industry with Starbucks offering Soya milk, and McDonalds offering salads. In New York, the city council has banned certain types of fats. The proportion of vegetarians has only increased slightly in the last 20 years, with just over 5% of UK adults reporting themselves to be vegetarian in 2004. However, the number of food venues offering vegetarian options due to its association with healthy eating has increased exponentially along with a perception that vegetarian food in restaurants is more than 'vegetable lasagne' or a 'cheese omelette'. Restaurants are also aware of specialist diets, whether it is catering for gluten free or the Atkins diet. Consumers will even visit a food nutritionalist or advisor of seek opinion about 'food balance' or 'sensitivity towards certain foods'. The specialist diet is becoming more mainstream with individuals avoiding certain foodstuffs like 'dairy products' or the promotion of detox diets to cleanse the body. Consumers are therefore becoming ever more demanding and cautious regarding the food they eat. These concerns and fears can be exploited in order to maximise potential marketing of certain products. However, due to the volatile nature of demands and trends, these requirements are hard to predict. Food providers need to have 'quick response' mechanisms in place to enable them to keep up with dietary fads and health scares.

PANI PURI/GOLGAPPA/GOLGAPPE - INDIAN STREET SNACK

Panipuri or Gol Gappa or Gup chup is a popular street snack in the Indian sub-continent. It comprises a round, hollow puri, fried crisp and filled with a watery mixture of tamarind, chilli and potato. The name panipuri literally means "water in fried bread". The snack has three major ingredients - Puris, pani (water) and stuffing.

1. Puris - Ready made puris can also be used.

Ingredients:

Maida or all purpose flour - 1 cup

Sooji (rava) - 1 tbl spn

Oil

Salt

Method

Mix flour, sooji and salt. Add sufficient water to make the dough. Keep it aside for half an hour.

Make small balls of the dough, roll it into tiny puris (make it to chapathi size and cut into small puris) and deep fry them in oil.

2. Pani

Ingredients

Coriander leaves - 3/4 cup

Green chillies - 3-4

Ginger - 2 pieces

Cumin(jeera) seeds - 1 tea spn

Jaggery - 1 tbl spn

Dates (Khajoor) - 7-8

Tamarind extract(thick) - 1 and 1/2 tea spn

Salt

Method

Grind all the ingredients together to a thick chutney. This chutney can be preserved for 2-3 days. While serving, dilute it with water to required consistency(do not make it too watery).

3. Stuffing

Ingredients

Sprouted moong - 1 cup

Onion (finely chopped) - 1/2 cup

Sev (Indian delicacy)- 1/2 cup

Method

Wash the sprouted moong to remove as much skin as possible. Then cook with 3/4 tea spn salt and about 3/4 cup of water. Serve puris with pani, onions, sev and cooked moong.

How to eat

Stuff the puris with moong, onions and sev (1 : 1/2 : 1/2 proportion). Pour pani in the stuffed puri. Enjoy!

PESARATTU - ANDHRA PRADESH

Pesarattu is a thicker verison of Dosa made specifically in major towns of Andhra pradesh.

Ingredients

Whole Moong dall - 2 cups

Rice - 4 table spoons

Onions - 3 finely chopped

Green chillies - 6 finely chopped

Red chillies - 2

Ginger - small piece

Cumin seeds - 1/2 t.spoon

Cilantro - 1 bunch finely chopped

Salt - 1.5 t.spoons

Cooking Oil for making Pesarattu

METHOD

1. Rinse and soak whole moong dhall and rice in water for 4 hours.
2. Grind the above with green chilles, red chillies, ginger, cumin seeds, salt and little onion.
3. Fry the remaining onions in oil and keep them aside.
4. Make the Pesarattu like dosas, and put a spoon full of onions on the dosa and fold the dosa before serving.
5. Serve with coriander chutney or onion chutney.

IDLY - KANCHEEPURAM

The idli is a savory cake popular throughout South India. The cakes are usually two to three inches in diameter and are made by steaming a batter consisting of fermented black lentils (de-husked) and rice.

Kancheepuram Idli as the name goes is from Kancheepuram, a holy city in Tamilnadu, India. History goes that Kancheepuram Idly is served as prasadam (offering) in Varadharaja Perumal Temple, a famous Hindu temple dedicated to Lord Vishnu, located in the Kancheepuram. It is a huge Idli (Steamed Rice Cake) which is added with spices.

INGREDIENTS

Raw rice - 2 cups

Whole black gram - 2 cups

Oil - 5 tblsp

Ghee- 4 tsp

Whole black pepper - 2 tsp

Thick curd - ½ litre or 500 gms

Cooking soda - ¼ tsp

Cumin seeds - 2 tsps

METHOD

1. Soak dhal and rice together for 3 hours.

2. Grind this after soaking till it reaches a coarse consistency. Batter should be thick preferably. Allow it to ferment for 10 -5 hours.
3. Before pouring the batter into idli plates for steaming, add oil, ghee, pepper, cumin seeds, curds and soda to the batter.
4. Grease idli plates and pour batter as in normal idlis but a bit thicker.
5. Steam till the idlis are cooked. This will take approximately 35- 45 minutes.
6. Serve hot along with idli chilli powder mixed with oil.

Note: You can make plate idlis if you want to add excitement to your idlis. Instead of the normal idli plates, grease and steam in bigger plates to make 4 or 5 plate idlis.

Okinawa is a prefecture, or island, that is located in Japan. It is considered to be the largest island in population as well as in size. There are a number of islands that make up the Okinawa Prefecture. Some are famous for their beaches while others are known for their beautiful jungle atmosphere. The climate of Okinawa is hot, making it the perfect place to visit for those looking towards a tropical vacation.

TRADITIONAL CUISINE

Okinawan cuisine is extremely different from the cuisine normally served in Japan. Okinawa has a different climate and vegetation, which means that it is nothing like the food available on the mainland. Most people in Okinawa exist on whole grains and vegetables. Meat is served, but not extremely often. Of the meat that is served, Spam, Soki (a type of pork spare rib) and other pork meat are the favorites. Both white rice and brown rice are served, as well as noodles, but that is truly the only similarity between Japanese and Okinawan dishes.

Traditional Dishes

One traditional dish is chanpur. Chanpur is a stir fry dish that is made in a number of different ways. Each way is slightly different, but each way has vegetables, tofu and a type of meat or fish in it. Sometimes pork belly is used as the meat, other times tuna is. One favorite is Gy chanpur. This is made with a bitter melon (known as the gy melon), as well as other vegetables, tofu, Spam and bacon. Other chanpur is made with pasta and eggs.

Okinawa soba is a dish that is so popular in Okinawa, it was named after the country. It is a noodle soup that is made using thick wheat noodles. The noodles are then topped with either scallion, pork belly, pork ribs, pickled ginger or a fish cake. Often diners add Korean pepper to the dish in order to spice it up. Okinawa soba can be found in almost any restaurant on the island.

Another popular dish is taco rice. Taco rice is begun with a base of rice. Lettuce is then laid on top of the rice and taco meat is piled on top of that. Cucumber, cheese and tomato are crumbled over the mixture to complete it. Sometimes the dish is served in a tortilla roll. This meal is served frequently for lunch and is found in many school cafeterias.

Drinks

Awamori is an alcoholic beverage that is made only in Okinawa. It is created by distilling rice. This drink is exported to Japan, although the exported brands are not as strong as those that stay inside the country. It is also sometimes called island sake.

Food in Oceania

Oceana is the section of the world located in the Pacific oceans. It includes a number of different countries, as well as small volcanic islands that have no names. Some of the countries that reside in Oceana are Australia, Indonesia, Samoa, Solomon Islands, Marshall Islands, and New Zealand.

TRADITIONAL CUISINE

Because there are so many different islands, each with a different culture inhabiting it, there is no one cuisine that is shared by them all. There are some common ingredients and spices that some of the islands share between them, but the dishes are extremely varied in flavor as well as texture.

Fish

One ingredient that is shared by many of the islands is fish. There is an abundant supply of fish that surrounds these islands, and the natives learned to make use of the surplus by creating delicious meals that centered on the protein without becoming boring. When served plain, fish is often grilled whole and served in the middle of the table for guests to pick at. Sometimes fish is chopped up and a fish base is created for a stew or soup, while other times it is served raw in the form of sashimi or sushi.

Coconuts

Coconuts are found on a number of the tropical islands. They grow wild and are usually found in abundance. Natives on the islands figured out a number of different ways to use the coconut. Coconut meat can be eaten plain or can be used to garnish dishes. Many use coconut meat in desserts such as cookies or cakes. Coconut milk has saved more than one starving lost person in the islands. It is extremely nutritious and is one of the few things that people can drink when in a foreign country without having to worry about getting any parasites. Coconut milk is used in a number of different dishes on the island. It is sometimes used to sweeten a stew or soup, and other times is used to marinate a meat in. Coconut milk has a way of softening up a piece of meat that not many marinades do.

OTHER DISHES

Many of the islands in Oceana that are close to Asia use rice and noodles, just as the Asian culture does. The starches are a staple in the diet, served with almost every meal. One dish that is popular is called nasi goreng. Nasi goreng is created when fried rice is mixed with other items. Sometimes the leftovers from the night before are thrown into the dish and it is served for breakfast. Chicken is also cooked frequently on the islands. Some islands spice the chicken up and grill it, while others make a type of chicken soup out of it. Many of the island chickens are allowed to run wild and are skinnier and have more muscles because of it.

Food in North America

North America is an extremely diverse culture. Some call it a melding pot, because many people immigrated to the continent from other cultures. Many French immigrants settled in Canada, but while the French influence is still there, it has been diluted over centuries of other cultures finding their home in the beautiful wilderness as well. The Mexican people have a more tightly-knit culture, as their ancestors passed down the "old ways" successfully to the younger generation. The United States is extremely diverse, with older traditions staying in the east and newer traditions popping up in the west.

Canada

Canadian cuisine began with the French but has since morphed to include some of other cultures, including those of Great Britain and the United States. Those living in the province of Quebec still tend to cook French food. Their dishes are hearty fare that has simple flavors, all of which meld together well. In the wilds of the North, game is much more popular and is eaten on a regular basis. One can get caribou, moose or venison without much trouble. Smoked meat is delicious in Canada, especially in the city of Montreal. Salmon is on the menu frequently, especially when visiting either coast of the country.

Mexico

Traditional Mexican food has been handed down through generations of family members. It was created by using the available resources, which means that many of the dishes are very spicy. This is because spices were always plentiful in Mexico. Spanish rice is familiar to most. It is a dish created by blending garlic, tomatoes, onions and a few other spices in with white rice. The result is a spicy rice that goes perfect as an appetizer.

Chicken is popular in the southern area of Mexico, while beef is the main protein in the northern area. Both areas make a version of burritos. This meal is a filing one that uses thin tortilla's as a base. Some put rice in the tortilla, others put meat, and still some use leftover beans as a way to be economical. Burritos had their start as a way to eat food cheaply and easily, but have now become extremely popular in many parts of the world.

The United States

When people immigrated to the United States hundreds of years ago, they settled on the east coast. This may be why most of the food in the east coast is more reminiscent of the past than the food in the west coast is. In the east, the food tends to be very filling and warm. This may be because of the difficult and long winter months. Stews are extremely popular, as are other dishes that can be combined in one pot, such as casseroles. Beef and chicken are the two most popular proteins. In the northeast, citrus has to be shipped in from the south or the west, as there is not a long enough growing season for it to thrive.

Those in the west coast live on a much lighter fare. People moving to the west from the east met people from other cultures and integrated their food into the recipes they currently had. This made a new type of food called fusion, which is when foods from two different cultures are meshed together. Fruit is popular in the west because it grows so well in the bright sunshine.

FOOD IN MIDDLE EAST

The Middle East is located in south-western Asia, between Europe and North Africa. It is an area that has suffered from a number of wars, sometimes devastating the countries that lie in the beautiful area. The cuisine in the Middle East ranges from light, tasty fares to heavier, more filling foods. Some of the ingredients that are used in a majority of the countries include sesame seeds, chickpeas, pitas and honey.

Savory Foods

Some countries in the Middle East, such as Egypt, prefer to eat savory foods that are full of herbs and spices. Lamb is a protein that is often used in the Middle East as it is plentiful. Many of the cultures mix sweet foods with lamb in order to dilute the gamey taste a bit. Vegetables are also used frequently in Middle Eastern cuisine. In Israel and in Egypt, vegetables such as eggplant or peppers are stuffed with mixtures, such as rice and beef or rice and beans. Beans, such as fava beans, are used as a base for many dishes. In Egypt fava beans are mashed and mixed with garlic and olive oil in order to make a dish called ful medames, which is eaten in the morning.

The Pita

Pita bread is eaten quite often in the Middle East. It is a soft bread that is shaped in a circle. The center is hollow, and when the bread is cut in half, a pocket is opened and ingredients are stuffed into the pocket. This makes the sandwich very easy to make and enjoy. Many Middle Eastern countries use the pita to put falafel in. Falafel is a meat product that is often eaten as a quick meal or snack. Pitas were first created in the Middle East but have since become used throughout the world. Some cultures stuff deli meats into the pocket while others prefer vegetables or tuna fish.

Couscous

Couscous is another dish that is found in a majority of the Middle Eastern countries. Couscous is a dish that is created when small wheat granules are coated in wheat flour. The granules are then steamed in either water or a flavored broth. There are a number of ways that this dish can be served. Some countries serve it plain while other countries mix vegetables or meat, such as lamb, into the dish before serving. Couscous has also become popular in the West where it is available to purchase in a box mix.

FAST FOOD

Fast food is available to purchase in the Middle East. Some countries have fast food stands, such as McDonalds, that are available to eat in, while others rely on outdoor vendors. Most of these vendors are extremely sanitary, but tourists should always insist that the food is created in front of them so that they know that the food they are eating is fresh. Kebobs are often found at roadside vendors, as are falafel sandwiches.

Food in Hawaii

One of the most popular vacation spots, Hawaii is known for its beautiful beaches and its amazing vistas. There are nineteen separate volcanic islands that are attached to the name, and each one has its own perks. The most popular island is called Hawaii, much like the state is, but goes by "The Big Island" in order to avoid confusion. It is home of some of the major resorts and is also home to the most active volcano in the world. Oahu and Maui are the next most popular islands. Waikiki beach is on the island of Oahu and is one of the most popular beaches in the world. Maui is home to a tall crater named Haleakala.

Traditional Cuisine

The cuisine of Hawaii is hard to define. It is a mixture of foods that were brought by the many different types of immigrants that settled on the islands. The dishes created make the best use of the flora and fauna on the island, as well as the animals that were imported there. Local ingredients include things like yams, coconuts, mussels, fish, seaweed, bananas, breadfruit and taro. A number of ingredients are regularly imported onto the islands such as soy sauce, Spam, tofu, wasabi, melons and fish sauce.

Traditional Dishes

A plate lunch is often the first things that tourists find when they begin to eat in the islands. This is a lunch that generally consists of a few scoops of rice, a macaroni salad that is made very simply with just macaroni and mayonnaise, and a choice of toppings. Some of the toppings include gravy, hamburger and a fried egg. The dish is served in the majority of restaurants, especially those on the Big Island.

One dish that has made it to the mainland of the United States is poke. Poke is a fish salad that is created by slicking up one-inch cubes of a number of vegetables, seaweed and fish. It is served as an appetizer. This dish is often purchased, even by the locals, at a supermarket or a fish hut. Most stores have a variety of different types of poke to choose from.

Mahi-mahi is a food that most tourists try before they leave the island. The Mahi-mahi is a fish that is also called the "dolphin fish". This fish has a sweet taste and is similar to a swordfish. It is enjoyed by many different cultures because it is both kosher, for Jewish people, as well as halal, for Muslims. This is because it has scales as well as fins through its entire life.

Loco moco is another popular Hawaiian dish. It begins with white rice which is then covered with a hamburger patty. A fried egg goes on top of the hamburger and gravy gets poured over the entire thing. This dish became popular when the American soldiers were stationed on the islands. So popular, in fact, that many of them brought the recipe home with them. It is now

Food in Europe

The area of Europe is a large area that is located between Asia, Africa, and the Arctic. Europe is often visited by tourists. Some head to see the culture of France or the United Kingdom, while others head to Spain, Greece or Italy in order to enjoy the warm weather and the beautiful beaches.

Traditional Cuisine

Europe is considered to be the cultural center of fashion, interior design, and cuisine. The only problem with this statement is that what is considered to be high fashion, great interior design and delicious cuisine varies from country to country. The cuisine in Europe, no matter which country is visited, is almost always delicious. Gourmet cooking has become a fine art, and visitors to the area can find almost any type of food, from Italian to Spanish to Chinese, no matter which country they are visiting.

Heavier Foods

The cooler climates tend to serve the heavier foods. England, Belgium, Ireland, Germany and Hungary are just a few of the countries that boast of a heavy fare for the casual traveler. Countries that are mostly landlocked, such as Hungary and the Czech Republic, learned how to create filling meals on very little. In Hungary, goulash is a meal that is found on almost every menu. Some consider it to be the national dish. Goulash is made by first browning meat in a skillet. Water is then added to the skillet along with onions, peppers and garlic. Sometimes potatoes are added as a way to thicken the broth. This hearty dish is served with mashed potatoes.

People in these cold climates needed to create foods that kept them warm and kept them full, so that they could work a long day without having to worry about food. This is why heavy sauces and thick stews are so popular. Those used to a lighter fare may have a hard time adjusting to some of these meals. In the United Kingdom, for instance, some consider it sacrilegious to serve a shank of meat without adding a gravy to it.

Lighter Fare

Food in the Mediterranean, which includes countries such as Greece, Monaco, Italy and Spain, generally has a much lighter feel to it. Emphasis is placed more on blending the tastes together rather than in creating a filling meal. In many of these countries, it is considered rude to not be served at least three courses during a full dinner setting. Coffee is also an important part of the Mediterranean culture. Espresso is a favorite coffee drink, as is cappuccino and caffe late. These drinks have migrated over into the Western cultures to become extremely popular. People that eat a Mediterranean diet generally eat a number of fruits and vegetables, as well as fish. Heavier meats are eaten, but are generally served in thin slices, not large chunks.

WHAT IS FOOD TOURISM

It used to be that people traveled to distant lands in order to see historic monuments or to have an adventure. Now, however, some people are heading to distant lands in order to eat historic food or have a culinary adventure. Food tourism is sweeping the world and is becoming something that everyone should know and understand. But what, exactly, is food tourism

Food Tourism

We have all seen the little tourist center at the popular vacation destinations. You walk in and the guide will help you to find the best lodging, shopping, and things to do in the area. Thesc tourist centers are a great help to someone who is unfamiliar to the area and just wants to enjoy the sites. But what about people who traveled to the area specifically to try the cuisine

Culinary shows have become the rage in most parts of the world. Shows like "Ramsey's Kitchen Nightmares", and "Top Chef", are helping ordinary people to understand the ins and outs of all types of cuisines. Cookbook sales have gone through the roof, all because people want to attempt to recreate the dishes that they see on these television shows.

Reasons to Visit

Some people believe that instead of trying to recreate a dish, they should go to the country that is famous for it. Take, for instance, John. John enjoyed eating Chinese takeout from the local fast-food Chinese restaurant. One day John decided that he wanted to see what traditional Chinese food was like, so he hopped a flight over and spent a week traveling the country, trying different foods. It might sound a bit incredible, but this type of a situation is occurring more and more regularly.

One survey found that one in six of 150 million United States tourists took a food tour or tried a cooking class in another country while they were on vacation. Some of those people actually traveled to their destination spot just to try the specific cuisine. There have been people that have traveled to New York City in order to eat from one end of the Big Apple to the other, and those who have gone "down under" just to have a steak off the infamous "barbie".

Planning a Trip

Food tourism is something that is becoming more commonly understood. But how would someone decide where to go, and what to see It's fairly simple, actually. Tourists should first decide which type of cuisine they would like to try. Start by figuring out which food they love the best and by doing a little research. Then, after the tourist arrives in the city, they should seek the advice of others. Ask the local cab driver or the hotel clerk where the best places are to eat. Don't think that you have to stick to gourmet restaurants. Sometimes the smaller restaurants that are on the side streets are the best places to try traditional cuisine.

Food in Egypt

Egypt is a large country in Africa that is connected to Asia by the Sinai Peninsula. It has long been known for being the home of Egyptian civilization, with mysterious pyramids, spooky mummies and interesting hieroglyphs. Cairo is the destination of most tourists, as it is the home of not only the Egyptian Museum, but the Giza Pyramids as well. Luxor is where the gateway to the Valley of the Kings lies, and Siwa is a hidden oasis town that has much to offer it's visitors. Egypt is truly a country that caters to adventurers and casual travelers alike.

Traditional Cuisine

Like much of the eastern Mediterranean countries, traditional Egyptian cuisine consists of many different herbs and spices. Lamb is the popular protein and vegetables are often stuffed and eaten as a side dish.

Traditional Dishes

One dish that is considered to be the national dish of Egypt is called ful medames. Ful medames is a dish that is usually eaten for the breakfast meal. Fava beans are cooked in a copper pot extremely slowly and for a long period of time. This makes the beans easy to mash. After they have been mashed, olive oil and garlic is added. Onion, garlic and lemon juice are also used to season the mashed fava beans. Baladi bread is sometimes served along side the dish, as well as hard boiled eggs and other vegetables.

Shawerma is another popular Egyptian dish. It is a sandwich that is made up using either lamb, chicken or goat. A large piece of meat is skewed with onion and tomato on top. It is roasted for a number of hours. The meat is then shaved off in thin slices and is put into a pita bread or other flatbread. Sometimes hummus, Amba sauce or pickled vegetables are put into the bread. It is often eaten as fast food and is available on a number of carts around the larger cities. Dukkah is another quick snack. It is a mixture that is created using nuts, seeds and other spices. Often pita bread is dipped into olive oil and then the mixture. This gives the bread a different taste and is extremely nutritious to eat.

Kushari is a popular dish and is served in most of the restaurants in the country. Kushari is created using a base of lentils, chickpeas, macaroni and rice. These are topped with garlic and tomato sauce and fried onions are often put on top. It is similar to the Western spaghetti and meatballs meal, but has a much more spicy taste.

FOOD IN DENMARK

Denmark is a small country located in Northern Europe. It used to be the home of the Vikings, which meant that it was a major power in Europe. Now, however, Denmark is a modern nation that is helping with the economic integration of Europe. Most tourists head to Copenhagen, which is one of the major cities of the country. Others head to Legoland, which is perfect for families or Lego-lovers to visit, and Ribe, the oldest town in Denmark.

Traditional cuisine

Traditional Denmark cuisine is much like the cuisine of Norway and Germany. Most dishes are very heavy and have a lot of meat and carbohydrates in them. People survived on the foods that they could grow until the 1860's, when Denmark finally became a member of trade with other nations. This means that vegetables and fruits played a large part in the majority of early dishes.

Traditional Dishes

The first meal of the day is usually buttered bread that is served with cheese, jam and coffee. Sometimes salami is served as well. Some Danish people eat cereal with a crumbled bread on top, or an porridge. On a special occasion, morgenbord is served. This is a buffet of different foods that are laid out during an anniversary or birthday. It will have a number of different breakfast selections on it.

Smorrebrod is a type of sandwich that is eaten during the lunch hour. It is a buttered rye bread that is topped with cold cuts, meat or cheese. There are a number of different combinations that can be made, but all of these open sandwiches are created using a base of a dark buttered bread and a meat or cheese. Just like the Danish have a special celebratory meal for breakfast, so do they for lunch. Kolde bord, or cold table, is a smorgasbord of lunch items that are served on a large table. Different items, such as pickled herring, Danish sausage, Veal medallion, cold cuts, and different breads, are laid out for people to choose from.

Dinner is the main meal of the day, and is when the family gathers together. Regular dinners may include dishes such as frikadeller. Frikadeller are a Danish meatball that is made using ground veal or pork, onions, eggs, and spices. It is made into balls, flattened, and fried in pork fat. They are often served with potatoes and gravy or red cabbage. These are also a popular dish in a smorgasbord.

Christmas Lunch

Christmas time is a special time in a Danish household. A Christmas lunch is often served. This lunch can be for family members or for a business. It includes traditional smorgasbord items, such as liver, cold cuts, salads, cheeses, and fruit. One thing that separates a Julefrokost from a traditional lunch buffet is the selskabssang, or party song. These are songs that are sung during the meal, making the occasion extremely festive."The industry needs to take note and use the opportunity to its advantage. Holidaymakers want a hands-on experience and food is a manifestation of a destination's culture.

"You can open a different door with every meal."

"The last five years has seen an incredible shift in the way holidays are marketed and it's all because people are demanding authentic experiences, said Erik Wolf, president of the International Culinary Tourism Association, a non-profit group representing more than 500 tourism businesses in 19 countries." For the first time, the true extent of food tourism has been measured in the UK by World Travel Market, the premier business event for the international travel and tourism industry, with research revealing more than half (53%) ranked eating traditional dishes as a 'very important' or 'important' part of their holiday.Meanwhile, a staggering 86% of Brits quizzed said they enjoyed local foods when abroad. The trend is not just limited to those on specialist tailor-made breaks either, with 83% of people who typically go on half- or full-board holidays admitting they willingly miss meals in their hotel or resort to try out local restaurants.

International chef Gary Rhodes, whose TV programmes has helped open up the world's traditional dishes and ingredients to a hungry audience, has recently opened a Rhodes restaurant in Calabash, on the Caribbean island of Grenada and onboard P&O Cruises' new liner Arcadia. He said: "The potential for tourism through dining is enormous and what better way to learn about a country than at the table! My experience is that travellers are becoming both more sophisticated and daring about what they eat."

Changes in Weekly Shop

Supermarkets have played a major part in the shift in attitudes, making foreign foods more available. One supermarket chain, Waitrose, for example, recently unveiled a range of tapas and Greek dishes that customers might have tried on their holiday. "The world is becoming a smaller place and we are seeing our customers' tastes change to reflect this. Dishes from all corners of the globe are becoming mainstream additions to the British dinner table," said Waitrose communications manager Gill Smith."Flavours people have sampled on holiday are becoming more popular.

As they travel to further afield, customers are more willing to experiment with new flavours. Our oriental range now extends beyond Chinese dishes to Japanese, Malaysian and Thai foods. "We're also finding that as people travel more, they are more knowledgeable about regional trends within countries. Instead of simply wanting Indian foods, we're finding that customers are aware of Goan and Keralan food and want to buy these dishes at their local supermarket." In the research, the growing trend to change what they put in their supermarket trolley because of holiday experiences is evident. A total of 42% said this affected their weekly shop choices.Wolf said that some tourist offices are beginning to highlight food as a way of promoting their country to foreign visitors. This trend though must grow still further.

Chicago Led the Way

Chicago led the way eight years ago when it appointed former chef Judith Hines as director of culinary arts and events. She oversees 275 annual food-related events, including its summer-long Stirring Things Up festival (May 1-Oct 31), which features culinary tours, food festivals, farmers' markets and concerts. Special hotel rates are available to visitors during the period.

Although it's impossible to know how many visitors are drawn by food alone, Hines said millions come for the festivals, including the 11-day Taste of Chicago in July, where 3.5 million people consumed 70,000 pounds of ribs and 250,000 slices of pizza last year. That helped boost hotel occupancy to 90% last summer. "Food certainly helps boost tourism. While cultural events like theatre might be a good hook for tourists, it won't appeal to all; the attraction of food is universal" said Hines. "The misperception is that it has to be all five-star fine dining. We have 76 different ethnic neighbourhoods and promote them all. Having really authentic food is part of the attraction."

Chicago's focus on food includes a food concierge in one of the city's largest tourist offices adjacent to a large theatre booking agency. "It's a great tie-up. We explain the food scene to people who are looking for somewhere to eat on their night out." Hines also offers city tours with a difference, with a bus stopping at four local restaurants with diners having a course in each. "It's a fun way to find out about the city's culture and heritage," she explained. Operators claim the last five years has seen a significant change in the eating habits of Brits abroad, with clients shunning the 'chips with everything' restaurants and seeking out more local flavours.This is borne out by World Travel Market's independent research which indicated that 62% of those questioned shunned "glamorous" foreign restaurants and wanted to eat in rustic surroundings with the locals. Only 7% said they would prefer to eat in glamorous surroundings when overseas. Only 15% of those questioned would plump for international cuisine rather than food typical of the area in which they were staying.

Demand for Authentic Experience

"People want an authentic experience," claimed Chris Orme, general manager of Far East specialist Travel Indochina. "We are talking much more about food to people when they book and make it a central part of the holiday, going to local restaurants and experimenting. The availability of Chinese, Thai and Vietnamese food in the UK means clients want to try the authentic stuff much more. "People have booked particular holidays with us on the strength of the food. We're certainly not an operator that deals with food tours, but eating has certainly become a big interest for our clients."

Long Travel, a specialist in rural Italy and Sicily, claimed around 85% of its clients now asked specifically for food advice when booking. Contracts manager Laura Bell said: "Customers have very high expectations of the food in Italy because it receives so much good press and is always featured in cookery programmes."Getting back to nature and trying out dishes in a traditional setting is a must for our clients. Even the larger hotels we use grow many of their own vegetables and produce wine now."

Restaurant Concierge Service

Mercedes Fehler, marketing manager at upmarket specialist Harlequin Worldwide said demand for local cuisine was so high among its customers the operator had introduced a 'restaurant concierge' service. Customers can contact the operator before departure and the concierge will recommend and make reservations at restaurants around the globe.

"The concierge contacts the hotel the customer is staying in to get advice about the places to eat nearby and will make bookings. It's a very popular service in long-haul destinations," said Fehler. "Short haul, people tend to get out and look themselves. Hunting around for a place to eat in Europe is something people are more comfortable with."

Meanwhile, Caribbean specialist Carib Tours runs a 'food evening' each year for regular clients to showcase the best local restaurants. "People in the UK have access to some of the best restaurants in the world and so they won't settle for poor food when they're away," said Carib Tours managing director Paul Cleary.

"The four aspects of a holiday that are important to our clients are weather, beach, luxury and food. "The trend in the Caribbean has been for 'big name' European restaurants and chefs to open in the last few years. Clients want to eat in them, maybe as a special occasion. They also want to get out and eat locally. In Barbados, the Oistin's Fish Fry is a great example, but then it also has The Cliff, one of the world's best restaurants."

The DIY trend has even started to spread long-haul, according the Martin Grass, sales and marketing director of Rex Hotels., which has nine properties in the Caribbean and two in Kenya. "The Caribbean has been dominated by the big all-inclusives in the past and people had no need to go out to eat. While that is still very popular with the US market, people from the UK are a bit more adventurous, especially to the eastern Caribbean. Islands such as Barbados and Antigua have fantastic local restaurants and are seen as safe to venture out at night. The vast majority of our business from the UK is now room-only, because people want to sample the food and it is comparatively cheap to eat out."

But food has become a central part of the overseas marketing for nations around the world. Earlier this year,

Portugal teamed up with Harrods to promote its national dishes through the upmarket stores famous food hall. For the European destination, the message aims to attract not only those on traditional packages, but also the major villa holiday market predominantly served by the low-cost carriers, since these people eat out more.

Portuguese National Tourist Office director José António Preto da Silva said: "Our cuisine is now one of the key attractions for UK visitors, with each region of Portugal offering unique cooking style as well as local specialities. "Mealtimes are highly valued by the Portuguese, providing a leisurely opportunity to indulge in good food and good wine while catching up with family and friends, and this is a tradition we encourage visitors to join in to capture the true essence of our country and people."

The Rise of Food Festivals

Similarly, Singapore hosts an annual food festival each July celebrating a different aspect of its culture. This year (it's 14th) marks the 40th anniversary of the country's independence, majoring on what it is perhaps best known for by foreign visitors &endash; its hawker (street) food.

Tee Yen Chew, Singapore Tourism Board's Area Director for Northern & Western Europe said: "Singaporeans are passionate about food and eating. In almost every corner of the island, you will find an endless variety of food served hot or cold at any hour of the day or night. Singapore's cultural diversity is very much reflected in the variety of local food it has to offer &endash; Chinese, Malay, Indian, Peranakan and Eurasian. It is very important to communicate this to people thinking about visiting Singapore. It's not just a fusion of east and west, it the country's unique cultural tapestry."

Food Tourism Destinations

Some destinations have begun to realise that there is great potential for food tourism to offer a sustainable tourism product, whether it is the fine wines of California or the great cheeses of France. One of the best examples of food tourism has been the rise in prominence of Ludlow in the United Kingdom as a food tourism destination whether it is festivals, slow food or Michelin star restaurants.

Ludlow from the early beginning of a farmers market has prospered into a major food tourism destination with a density of high quality restaurants, an abundance of local food suppliers in the high street and food festivals and events to attract tourists. Ludlow as a food destination illustrates its success through:

- Using food as a means to create cultural capital and social cachet.
- Creating a density of food and drink suppliers which results in a tourism eating and shopping experience.
- Creating a local authentic promise based upon good quality and fair pricing.
- Creating a unique product better than that found in other regional food destinations.
- Producers seeing themselves as being involved in tourism.
- Tourism providers focusing on food as a point of difference.

Today, the consumer is better educated, wealthy, has travelled more extensively, lives longer, and is concerned about his health and the environment. As a result food and drink has become more important and have a higher priority amongst certain social groupings. Too the extent food is the new culture capital of a destination, as if culture has moved out of the museum to become a living experience of consumption. One thing is clear; food must be a quality product, whether it is slow food or fast food. Finally, if food is not for you, there is always the no-food movement which is all the rage in Japan where holiday-makers are flocking to the Arina Hotel in the idyllic Nagano Mountains for a fasting feast!

Chapter 2

Food Tourism Around the World

Visitors to Rome have long understood that among the city's highlights, ranking right up there with the Pantheon or the Colosseum, are its typical dishes. Some are seasonal (carciofi alla giudia, pizza con prosciutto e fichi), others are not (spaghetti alla gricia, trippa alla romana), still others could go either way (some fritti are, some are not).

With all this variety and seasonality on its side, Rome appears strongly rooted in tradition, impervious to change. But with roughly 9 million visitors annually and nearly 4 million residents in the metropolitan area, the city and its customs are threatened every day. Consumers demand out of season dishes, leading restaurants to serve them. Residents demand value and convenience, spurring the rise of supermarkets. Throw in globalization, a corrupt Minister of Agriculture, a farming crisis, and a shift in local food sensibilities, and Rome's gastronomic future is in serious trouble.

As a visitor (or resident for that matter), there are several things you can do to lessen your adverse impact on the city. Here are a few ways to become a responsible food tourist in Rome (and elsewhere!):

Don't shop at Supermarkets

If you are staying at a hotel, purchase your provisions at an alimentari (deli). If you are staying at a self-catering apartment, pick up your bread at the bakery, meat at the butcher, and produce at the produce market. Patronizing small local businesses will keep them alive as Despar, GS, Sma and other supermarkets exert their influence.

Avoid Chains and Franchises

Aside from the unfortunate presence of The Hard Rock Cafe, McDonalds, and Burger King, Rome has been rather resistant to American culinary imperialism. However, there are still a number of Italian chains operating in the center like the tragic Blue Ice gelateria, and Spizzico on the Via del Corso. They offer bad product made with terrible ingredients, chemical colorings, and preservatives. The Autogrill on major Italian roadways and food service at rail stations and on the trains themselves are also run by large corporations. Avoid! Prepare for a road trip or train travel by picking up some fresh sandwiches made at a locally owned alimentari.

Frequent Restaurants That Source Locally

In the past few years, a growing number of restaurants have been dedicated to using local products, from produce and olive oil to meat and cheese. Checchino dal 1887 (Via di Monte Testaccio, 30) and Palatium (via Frattina 94) have been at this for years, and now many other places are doing it, too. Back in June, I wrote this piece for the New York Times on locavore dining in Rome. In addition to the places mentioned in the article, the restaurant at Citta' dell'Altra Economia in Testaccio also serves food prepared with locally sourced ingredients.

Get Involved with the Rome Sustainable Food Project

The Rome Sustainable Food Project, based at the American Academy in Rome on the Janiculum Hill, is a joint venture between the AAR and Alice Waters that uses fresh, seasonal, organic products to create nourishing meals for the Academy's fellows and visiting scholars. A 50 euro donation to the Friends of the American Academy in Italy gives you the opportunity to have lunch at the AAR with up to 10 guests. Become a friend here.

Respect the Seasons

Just because you want a deep fried artichoke doesn't mean you get to have it. I recently got into this discussion on the Chowhound Italy board when I castigated someone for ordering carciofi alla giudia at Sora Margherita (one of the worst places around, by the way) in July. Another reader came to the offender's rescue, stating, "For those of us who are not in Rome year-round, the production of fried artichokes out of season even if from non-local artichokes is appreciated". This statement is wrong on so many levels. If you don't know when Roman artichokes are in season (February-May), that's one thing (see next tip), but if you knowingly order out of season dishes, you are being an irresponsible food tourist. Creating demand for out of season produce has significant ramifications, both for the local culture, as well as for the environment. If you must have a deep fried treat from the Roman Jewish tradition in July, pass on the carciofo alla giudia and indulge in fiori di zucca!

Learn the Seasons

With Rome's incredible biodiversity, it may seem intimidating to learn when each fruit and vegetable is in season. To make the process easier, take a spin in a produce market (Testaccio, San Giovanni di Dio, or Citta' dell'Altra Economia; NOT Campo de' Fiori which is one of the worst places on earth to see what's local or seasonal). Farmers markets like the Mercato di Campagna Amica del Circo Massimo (on hiatus until September) and the Roma Farmer's Market in the ex-Mattatoio are other destinations for finding what's local and in season.

Here is a list of some local produce and when to look for it:

Apples	August-November
Apricots	Junc-August
Artichokes (carciofi	

romaneschi IGP)	February-May
Asparagus	April-June
Beans	June-August
Black leaf kale	October-February
Broccoli	July-November
Cabbage	July-February
Carrots	July-October
Cauliflower	July-November
Celeriac	August-November
Celery	July-October
Cherries	May-June
Corn	August-October
Cucumber	July-October
Eggplant	July-September
Fennel	October-November
Figs	June-September
Grapes	September-October
Leeks	July-February
Lemons	October-June
Onions	July-December
Oranges	November-June
Peaches	June-August
Pears	August-October
Peas	May-August
Peppers	June-October
Plums	July-September
Potatoes	August-October
Strawberries	April-August
Tomatoes	July-October
Turnips	July-February
Zucchini	July-November

These tips should get you started on responsible food tourism in Rome, but they are equally valid for other cities. Let me know your thoughts and if I have missed anything!

VEGETARIAN EATING

What Different Forms of Vegetarians Eat

What a vegetarian can eat depends on what type of vegetarian they are. The main types are listed below. There are some people who call themselves vegetarians even though they eat fish, so it is worth checking.

If vegetarians do eat eggs, it is usually only free-range eggs. If you know that the eggs you are serving are free range, it will be helpful to indicate this on your menu

Those that eat cheese will often only eat vegetarian cheese, because typically cheese uses animal product during its production; however more and more cheeses, especially those made in Scotland, now use a vegetarian alternative. If you are sure the cheese you are serving was made using vegetarian rennet, it will be helpful to indicate this on your menu.

Octo-Lacto Vegetarian (The most popular definition, also known as Ovo-Lacto)

These people do not eat red meat, poultry, fish, or any products that have ingredients which are animal-based, such as gelatine. They do eat eggs, milk, yoghurt, vegetarian cheese, honey etc.

Lacto Vegetarian

Lactose-vegetarians do not eat any foods that involve the slaughter of animals. They don't eat eggs, but do eat vegetarian cheese, yoghurt and milk.

Demi-Vegetarian

Demi-vegetarians don't eat red meat or poultry, but they do eat fish, eggs, vegetarian cheese, and milk-based products.

Vegan

Vegans do not eat red meat, poultry, fish, or any products that have ingredients which are animal-based and they also will not eat any product that is derived from animals, i.e. cheese, butter, milk, cream, yoghurt, eggs, honey, whey, gelatine (vegetable gelatine is available and will be labelled as such), honey, isinglass (a fish product used to refine many wines and beers).

Fruitarian

A Fruitarian is somebody who believes that you should not kill any living thing to survive. Instead, they can only eat the fruit of plants that don't actually mean death to the plant. Their diet consists of only fruit, nuts, seeds and other plant matter that can be gathered without harming the plant.

Macrobiotic

The macrobiotic diet consists of mostly whole grains and beans, although it does include the eating of fish.

Care should be taken when preparing a meal for a vegetarian, because many find that exposure to even small amounts of animal ingredients can cause physical discomfort which can range from a slight stomach upset to headaches to vomiting and diarrhoea. To be on the safe side, if you have used utensils for animal ingredients, either wash them or use separate utensils for making food for your customer, and never grill veggie burgers right next to meat.

Catering for Vegetarians

Most vegetarians will be happy to work with you to devise a menu that you can fit into your busy schedule and that meets their dietary requirements. Simple food, well-prepared with good quality ingredients will always be appreciated.

There are some products that can be used as replacements for egg and dairy products:

As a binder, substitute for each egg:

1/4 cup (2 ounces) soft tofu blended with the liquid ingredients of the recipe, or

1 small banana, mashed, or

1/4 cup applesauce, or

2 tablespoons cornstarch or arrowroot starch

The following substitutions can be made for dairy products:

Soy milk, rice milk, potato milk, nut milk, or water (in some recipes) may be used.

Buttermilk can be replaced with soured soy or rice milk. For each Cup of buttermilk, use 1 cup soymilk plus 1 tablespoon of vinegar.

Crumbled tofu can be substituted for cottage cheese or ricotta cheese in lasagne and similar dishes.

Several brands of non-dairy cream cheese are available in some supermarkets and kosher stores.

Typical Vegetarian recipes (suitable for vegans and vegetarians and can be adapted for fruitarians):

Some vegetarian Recipes

1. Yellow and Green Split Pea Rice.
2. Hot Tattie scones with a Scottish vegetarian cheese.
3. Scottish crumpets.
4. Fresh Scottish Bannocks.
5. Vegetarian Aberdeen Butteries / Rowies.
6. Breakfast Cranachan.

Active Tourism is a special way to spend your vacations. It is a new travelling philosophy that combines adventure, ecotourism and cultural aspects of a discovery tour. Active tourism is low-impact, ecological, socially compatible and high quality. Active tourism has three major aims:

Recreation: distraction from daily working routine during vacations. Active tourism is fun and can provide you all the pleasure you can desire. Relax your mind and recharge your body energy by practising exercise and actively participating in your entertainment.

Education: An active tourist is eager to learn and wants to know closely another culture and way of living. Your vacations should broaden your horizons. Willingness to learn the language, eat the tipical food, value local traditions and respect foreign cultures and beliefs.

Benefit: Tourism not only brings advantages to visitors but also helps the local economy and promotes development of the visited land. Active tourism is low impact, ecologically and socially sustainable. Active tourism uses and values nature, protects biodiversity and offers work to people.

ACTIVE TOURISM MARKET

Active Tourism is the contrary of passive tourism. This travelling concept is also opposed to Mass Tourism in the sense that is small scale, low-impact, run and administrated locally. Active Tourism is socially and ecologically sustainable.

Active Tourism comprises Ecotourism in the sense of protection of Biodiversity and admiration of natural beauty. But Active Tourism not only values Nature, but it also aims to educate the human being, culturally and ecologically. The participation in mental activities and physical excercises is very important for enhancing our life experiencies. An active tourist tries to educate a good mind in a healthy body.

Active Tourism should not be confused with Action Tourism, which envolves many sports activities like hicking, mountain bike, cross country, bungee jumping and extreme sports. Active Tourism excludes activities and practises that are harmful to the environment and pose a threath to biodiversity and cultural structure. Many activities of Action Tourism are already offered at big scale by Mass Tourism. To guarantee protection of the environment, active tourism activities are carried out by local professional personel and under strict scientific supervision. The tour guides of Active Tourism have an academic degree in ecology, biology, ethnology, arquitecture, history or sociology. Active Tourism is not only a superficial change of image (greenwashing) but is fully committed to its principles and guidelines of operation.

The World Tourism Organization (UNWTO), based in Madrid, Spain, is a United Nations agency dealing with questions relating to tourism. It compiles the World Tourism rankings. The World Tourism Organization is a significant global body, concerned with the collection and collation of statistical information on international tourism. This organization represents public sector tourism bodies, from most countries in the world and the publication of its data makes possible comparisons of the flow and growth of tourism on a global scale. The official languages of UNWTO are Arabic, English, French, Russian, and Spanish.

Organizational Aims

The World Tourism Organization plays a role in promoting the development of responsible, sustainable and universally accessible tourism, paying particular attention to the interests of developing countries.

The Organization encourages the implementation of the Global Code of Ethics for Tourism, with a view to ensuring that member countries, tourist destinations and businesses maximize the positive economic, social and cultural effects of tourism and fully reap its benefits, while minimizing its negative social and environmental impacts.

UNWTO is committed to the United Nations Millennium Development Goals, geared toward reducing poverty and fostering sustainable development.

History

The origin of the World Tourism Organization stems back to 1925 when the International Congress of Official Tourist Traffic Associations (ICOTT) was formed at The Hague. Some articles from early volumes of the Annals of

Tourism Research, claim that the UNWTO originated from the International Union of Official Tourist Publicity Organizations (IUOTPO), although the UNWTO states that the ICOTT became the International Union of Official Tourist Propaganda Organizations first in 1934.

Following the end of the Second World War and with international travel numbers increasing, the IUOTPO restructured itself into the International Union of Official Travel Organizations (IUOTO). A technical, non-governmental organization, the IUOTO was made up of a combination of national tourist organizations, industry and consumer groups. The goals and objectives of the IUOTO were to not only promote tourism in general but also to extract the best out of tourism as an international trade component and as an economic development strategy for developing nations.

Towards the end of the 1960's, the IUOTO realized the need for further transformation to enhance its role on an international level. The 20th IUOTO general assembly in Tokyo, 1967, declared the need for the creation of an intergovernmental body with the necessary abilities to function on an international level in cooperation with other international agencies, in particular the United Nations. Throughout the existence of the IUOTO, close ties had been established between the organization and the United Nations (UN) and initial suggestions had the IUOTO becoming part of the UN. However, following the circulation of a draft convention, consensus held that any resultant intergovernmental organization should be closely linked to the UN but preserve its "complete administrative and financial autonomy".

It was on the recommendations of the UN that the formation of the new intergovernmental tourism organization was based. Resolution 2529 of the XXIVth UN general assembly stated:

The general assembly] believes that a formula that would allow agreement to be reached more readily among governments for the establishment of an internationa tourism organization of an intergovernmental, particularl to assist the developing countries would be:

(a) The conversion of the International Union of Officia Travel Organizations into an inter-governmenta organization through a revision of its statutes: (b) Th establishment of operational links between the Unite Nations and the transformed Union by means of formal agreement.

In 1970, the IUOTO general assembly voted in favor forming the World Tourism Organization (WTO), based c statutes of the IUOTO, and after ratification by th prescribed 51 states, the WTO came into operation c November 1, 1974.

Most recently, at the fifteenth general assembly 2003, the WTO general council and the UN agreed establish the WTO as a specialized agency of the UN. Th significance of this collaboration, WTO Secretary-Gene Mr. Francesco Frangialli claimed, would lie in "the increas visibility it gives the WTO, and the recognition that will accorded to. Tourism will be considered on an equal footi with other major activities of human society".

Secretaries-General of UNWTO

1975-1985 - Robert Lonati (France)

1986-1989 - Willibald Pahr (Austria)

1990-1996 - Antonio Enriquez Savignac (Mexico)

1998-2008 - Francesco Frangialli (France)

2008-present - Taleb Rifai S.G ad interim (Jordar

STRUCTURE

General Assembly

The General Assembly is the supreme organ of Organization. Its ordinary sessions, held every two years, attended by delegates of the Full and Associate Members well as representatives from the Business Council. It is the most important meeting of senior tourism officials and high-level representatives of the private sector from all over the world.

Regional Commissions

Established in 1975 as subsidiary organs of the General Assembly, the six Regional Commissions normally meet once a year. They enable member States to maintain contact with one another and with the Secretariat between sessions of the General Assembly, to which they submit their proposals and convey their concerns. Each Commission elects one Chairman and its Vice-Chairmen from among its Members for a term of two years commencing from one session to the next session of the Assembly.

Executive Council

The Executive Council's task is to take all necessary measures, in consultation with the Secretary-General, for the implementation of its own decisions and recommendations of the Assembly and report thereon to the Assembly. The Council meets at least twice a year. The Council consists of Full Members elected by the Assembly in the proportion of one Member for every five Full Members, in accordance with the Rules of Procedure laid down by the Assembly with a view to achieving fair and equitable geographical distribution. The term of office of Members elected to the Council is four years and elections for one-half of the Council membership arc hcld every two years. Spain is a Permanent Member of the Executive Council.

Committees

World Committee on Tourism Ethics Programme Committee Committee on Budget and Finance Committee on Market and Competitiveness Committee on Statistics and the Tourism Satellite account Sustainable Development of Tourism Committee Committee on Poverty Reduction

Committee for the Review of Applications for Affiliate Membership

Secretariat

The Secretariat is led by Secretary-General ad interim Taleb Rifai of Jordan, who supervises about 110 full-time staff at UNWTO's Madrid Headquarters. He is assisted by the Deputy Secretary-General. These officials are responsible for implementing UNWTO's programme of work and serving the needs of Members. The Affiliate Members are supported by a full-time Executive Director at the Madrid Headquarters. The Secretariat also includes a regional support office for Asia-Pacific in Osaka, Japan, financed by the Japanese Government.

Learn more about the culinary experiences on offer in Australia - the fun section of foodie heaven

Our chefs and winemakers have learnt from the best, then bent the rules for a food and wine style all of their own. They've turned Australia's sun-kissed produce into a melting pot of cuisine and award-winning wines. Whether you want a fresh seafood platter, a racy Riesling, a modern Asian-fused meal or a crocodile sausage, Australia is the place to be. As warm and welcoming hosts who really know our stuff, we guarantee you won't forget your mouthfuls with us.

Eight ways to experience Australia's food and wine

1. Get a taste of the Top End

Welcome to Darwin's Mindil Beach Sunset Market where you can sample the flavours of the Asia-Pacific in a balmy, tropical setting. The coconut palms are swaying in the sunset, and the smell of sizzling satay and spicy noodles is in the air. Held every Thursday night between May and October, these popular markets offer over 60 food stalls to sate your appetite while the sun goes down.

2. Explore grapes galore in the Yarra Valley

Just behind Melbourne's fringes is the Yarra Valley - a place of pristine beauty, crisp clean water and friendly ambience. Clustered behind its rolling hills are 55 wineries, ranging from small family-owned vineyards to the famous Chateau Yering and Domain Chandon. Dine in gourmet restaurants and taste pinot noir, chardonnay and sparkling in a world reminiscent of French and Italian wine growing regions.

3. Cellar hop in the Barossa

Sip wines from more than 60 cellar doors, including Yalumba, Wolf Blass and Peter Lehmann in Australia's wine capital. In the Barossa you'll get to meet the people behind the labels and talk to them about their craft. You can also match your favourite wine with locally made cheese on a food and wine trail, tour historic wineries, take a tutored tasting or learn cellar secrets in a wine masterclass. Of course, nothing beats a long lunch under the gum trees with a bottle of one of the region's flagship wines, Barossa Shiraz or Eden Valley Riesling.

4. Discover cool-climate wines in the Coal River

Enjoy pinot noirs, cabernets and medal-winning chardonnays in the scenic Coal River Valley, just a 10 minute drive from Hobart. Sample superb cool-climate wines at the cellar doors and taste fresh Tasmanian produce in vineyard restaurants. Soak up the water views and stop off at the historic village of Richmond before completing your idyllic day trip.

5. Wine and dine with water views in Bondi

Savour spectacular ocean views with your food in Bondi's many beachside eateries. Enjoy a gelato at the 1920s Bondi Pavilion or watch the sun go down with a cocktail at one of the acclaimed restaurants. At the cafes on Campbell Parade, Hall Street and clustered around Bondi's back streets, you'll find everything from tapas to the world's best brunch to classic fish and chips.

6. Wine down in the Swan Valley

Indulge in divine local produce and award-winning wines in Western Australia's oldest wine region, just a boat ride from Perth. Take in the vines, waterfalls and lush bushland on a cruise up the Swan River. Then hop off for cellar door tastings, a visit to one of the microbreweries and a vineyard or picnic lunch. The Swan Valley is also great for horse riding, cycling, golf, wildlife watching and heritage walks. Check out the antique shops, pubs and galleries in the historic village of Guildford before you head home.

7. Taste the tropics in and around Cairns

Feast on locally-grown bananas, paw-paws, mangos, pineapples and lychees in the 'exotic fruit bowl of the world' near Cairns. But more than fruit flourishes in the region's rich volcanic soils, green rainforest belt and clean tropical waters. Try seafood, game meats, freshly-made pasta and organic bush foods. Visit an organic permaculture orchard in the rainforest, dine on freshly-caught barramundi in Cairns or sample macadamias and coffee on plantations in the tablelands.

8. Taste Canberra's rural riches on the Poachers Trail

Visit cool climate wineries, country cafes, art galleries and craft studios on this self-drive through the Canberra countryside. This is a region where you can enjoy the fruits of country labour - a table laden with delicious food and a bottle of last year's vintage. Stay in a bed and breakfast where you sleep in crisp linen sheets and wake to bird song on the verandah. Buy handmade glassware and pottery from the galleries and taste wood smoked meats and homemade wine on a farm.

PHILIPPINE FOOD

The Spanish came, so did the Japanese. The Americans said "Hi!" and the the Chinese said "buy!" while the Arabs said "Salaam."

Yep, they all have come, gone, and settled down in the Philippines. So, what have they left Siesta time from the Spanish...check. Trading from the Chinese...noted. The Americans traded Spam and pudding while the Japanese, well, we've got lots of interesting historical sites now.

Kidding aside, the Philippine culture has always been described as "diverse" due to the many different influences by foreign settlers and occupation during it's younger years. The same description may also be used to describe another important part of Filipino culture: the cuisine.

When it comes to eating Filipino food, most tourists are pleasantly surprised to see how fast they can develop a taste for Filipino food. Neither too hot, nor spicy, the native dishes often come with an array of condiments both foreign and local for the diner's use.

Generally speaking, much of Filipino cuisinc are dishes adapted from the settlers then continually refined and "taste-tested" to suit Filipino tastes. Some recognizable as spawns of foreign cuisine, some, dishes inspired by resourceful minds, while some are meant to be eaten with eyes closed for the foreign tourist.

Let me give you a tour of things you can expect to see on the local menu:

Appetizers

Ginataang Kuhol - Ever eaten snails Kuhol (escargot to the French) are fresh water snails cooked in coconut cream and gabi leaves. To cat this dish, you're going to have to need a toothpick to poke and draw out the luscious flesh inside the snail shell.

Kilawin - Kilawin is the process of putting raw fish, shrimp, or oysters into a vinegar dip with onions, ginger, pepper and other spices. Tangy, yet very tasty.

Mangga at Bagoong- sliced green mangoes served with sautéed shrimp paste.

Gambas - sizzling shrimp on a hot plate with tomato sauce, garlic and chillies.

Chicharon - deep-fried, lightly salted pork rinds. Best eaten with vinegar mixed with garlic and chillies.

For your Main Dish: The Usual Favorites

Lechong Baboy--The Lechon (roasted pig) is a constant favorite among the fiesta loving Pinoys. It is basically a huge and succulent pig stuck on a bamboo spit roasted over an open fire. The crisp skin is the favorite part of most Pinoys so don't be surprised to see them rushing to be first in line to get the choicest and largest portions of the skin.

Kare-kare -- Derived from Spanish dishes, the Kare kare (pronounced as kareh kareh) consists of ox tripe and meat cooked in a peanut sauce served with vegetables and bagoong (sauteed shrimp paste.)

Sinigang : A method of cooking that Filipinos claim to be an "original," "Sinigang" refers to the process of cooking either pork, fish, shrimps or beef in tamarind broth. Other variants of this is the "sinigang sa bayabas" (guava soup) or "sinigang sa miso" (tofu soup usually used for fish.) All variants are characterized by a slightly sour taste. Sinigang is usually served with "patis" (fish sauce).

Adobo -- Chicken meat and pork cooked in an infusion of soy sauce, vinegar, herbs and spices. It keeps well, it may be eaten with bread or rice or simply be taken on its own as a snack.

Bulalo - Joints of beef and beef shank soup boiled for hours and mixed with ginger, chopped corn on the cob, and other greens. Usually comes with patis (fish sauce and native lemon, calamansi.) Don't be surprised to see your Pinoy friends trying to coax the bone marrow out of the bone. It's considered a local delicacy.

Laing - Wilted taro leaves cooked in coconut cream, coconut milk, and shrimps.

Bicol Express - Sounds like a train doesn't it Well, you'd feel like one on fire after you get a taste of this kicker from the Bicol province. Chopped up chilies cooked in coconut milk that could pack a whopper like you'd never believe.

Dishes for Gustatory Adventurers

Pinapaitan - Goat or deer innards boiled in a broth seasoned with goat bile, pepper and ginger. Served as soup, Pinapaitan could be a dish listed under "Acquired Tastes."

Balut - Fertilized duck egg. Boiled and eaten with salt, the balut has that "Fear Factor" element for all tourists in the country. Duck embryos in different stages of maturity (feathered or not), a lot of foreign guests have difficulty chewing on half formed ducklings.

Balut

Soup Number Five - bull testicle soup. Also believed to be a powerful aphrodisiac.

Dinuguan - Pork meat and innards cooked in a hearty pork blood stew. Best eaten with rice flour cakes called puto. Most visitors to the country kind of find it hard to eat black food. One good tip would be, just close your eyes.

Durian/Marang - "Smells like hell yet tastes like heaven." Oh yeah the bread fruit can be pretty notorious for its stinky smell but also famous for its rich, creamy taste...once you get over the smell that is.

Snacks and Desserts

The Philippines is well known for its delicious rice cake called the bibingka (rice cakes cooked with eggs, salted eggs, milk, and cheese.) suman (sticky rice puddings served with coconut and sugar) and the biko (sticky sweet rice cakes.)

Being a tropical island, most desserts are based on fruits to be found in the Philippines: ripe mangoes with sago palm, ripe bananas cooked in caramel and served with vanilla ice cream , leche flan (flan made with egg whites and milk with caramel syrup. Something like Crème Brulee.) and the king of all treats, the halo-halo (literally "mix-mix") made out of mixed beans and fruits served in a tall glass topped with shaved ice, purple yam, leche flan bits, purple yam ice cream, milk and sugar.

Half the fun of visiting any place is trying out the food. So why stick to foods you can get at home when you can try food that hold so much promise of a thousand gustatory delights.

Laoag City, Ilocos Norte: GO senatorial candidate Loren Legarda said the country should take advantage of the billion-dollar gastronomical tourism phenomenon now sweeping the world by promoting internationally its various delectable cuisines and delicacies.

"We can put food on the table of hungry Filipinos by getting a bigger slice of the earnings derived from food tourism and the export of our native delicacies," Loren said.

"Food can solve the hunger problem in more ways than one. At the same time, we will be reinforcing Filipino hospitality for which we are well-known worldwide," she said.

Legarda cited a recent survey of tourist perceptions made by the World Travel Market, which showed two-thirds of international travelers are somehow influenced by food and drink in their choice of destinations.

"Food tourism today is where eco-tourism was 20 years ago, according to this study. Thus, the Philippines should think of holding culinary festivals and in exporting more of our delicacies and processed food to tickle international taste buds," said Loren.

Loren said foreigners would find Philippine cooking to be regionally diverse, influenced both by the east and the west.

"There's the hot and spicy cuisine of Bicol, Mindanao's Malay-influenced offering and Pampanga and Bulacan's sweet and sour cookery, to name a few," she pointed out. The government can help cooperatives, as well as small and medium scale enterprises (SMEs), in exporting native delicacies through micro financing and by holding international food exhibitions.

The food industry, on its own and taken with the hotel and resort sectors in the country, can generate much-needed jobs to help ease poverty and hunger in the Philippines, said Loren.

She added that food tourism could go hand in hand with other forms of tourism being promoted in the Philippines, including historical, ecological and sports tourism.

Erik Wolf, president of the International Culinary Tourism Association, has said that 53 percent of tourists worldwide had ranked eating traditional dishes as a very important travel consideration.

He added that 83 percent of tourists typically miss meals in their hotels or resorts to try out local restaurants.

Cheese is another food for which Switzerland is known, especially since Switzerland has been producing cheese for many centuries. Whether at home or abroad, the best known cheeses are Emmental (also known as Swiss cheese), Gruyère, Sbrinz, Appenzell and Tête de Moine.

But there is more to Swiss cheese than these few types: there are more than 450 cheese-makers who produce these delicious ambassadors of Swiss culture. Swiss cheese is made of milk produced by cows that graze on our flower-strewn meadows and somehow, one can nearly taste the sun in our delicious cheeses.

The Switzerland Cheese Marketing AG (SCM) has been in charge of marketing, communication and advertising for Swiss cheese since 1998. Click on www.schweizerkaese.ch for recipes that involve cheese, as well as more information regarding the individual dairies.

Swiss regional cuisine leaves little to be desired. Nearly every region has its own specialty. Discover home-cooking Switzerland-style or go for the gold with haute cuisine, for which Switzerland is well known.

Let our chocolate melt in your mouth - savour the exquisiteness and immerse yourself in the magical, mythical world of Chocolat Frey.

Being in possession of the original recipe for traditional Swiss chocolate and being committed to comprehensive quality right down to the last detail, Chocolat Frey has worked its way up to the No. 1 spot on the Swiss chocolate market. But it is not just in Switzerland that people sweeten their day with fine chocolates from Chocolat Frey. Chocoholics in more than forty different countries on all five continents regularly indulge their addiction with Frey's melt-in-your-mouth creations.

Frey's Secret

A great tradition, years of experience, a passion for perfection and careful choice of the finest ingredients together conspire to make the chocolates made by Chocolat Frey a truly unique pleasure - one could almost say an unforgettable event! Let our chocolate melt in your mouth - savour the exquisiteness and immerse yourself in the magical, mythical world of Chocolat Frey.

From Cocoa Beans to Chocolate

Chocolat Frey takes quality very seriously indeed. Only chocolate made from the very best raw materials is good enough to bear the name Frey. This means that at every stage in the production process, from the sourcing and roasting of the cocoa beans to their processing to make chocolate, is performed and supervised by experienced chocolatiers. So the really essential ingredients in Frey's 100% Swiss premium chocolate are choice raw materials, an indefatigably innovative spirit and highly skilled employees.

East of England, or better known as East Anglia, is one of the oldest and historically most heavily populated regions across the UK. The rich soil made it an agricultural paradise, bringing with it extensive development and historic artefacts that span the recorded history of England.

Travelling across the East of England allows visitors to explore a rich cultural heritage, see scenic estates and castles, and taste many traditional flavours. A great weekend getaway could entail a visit to Woburn Abbey, a succulent dinner of prime venison, and an evening at one of the many local breweries.

FOOD IN OCEANIA

Oceana is the section of the world located in the Pacific oceans. It includes a number of different countries, as well as small volcanic islands that have no names. Some of the countries that reside in Oceana are Australia, Indonesia, Samoa, Solomon Islands, Marshall Islands, and New Zealand.

Traditional Cuisine

Because there are so many different islands, each with a different culture inhabiting it, there is no one cuisine that is shared by them all. There are some common ingredients and spices that some of the islands share between them, but the dishes are extremely varied in flavor as well as texture.

Fish

One ingredient that is shared by many of the islands is fish. There is an abundant supply of fish that surrounds these islands, and the natives learned to make use of the surplus by creating delicious meals that centered on the protein without becoming boring. When served plain, fish is often grilled whole and served in the middle of the table for guests to pick at. Sometimes fish is chopped up and a fish base is created for a stew or soup, while other times it is served raw in the form of sashimi or sushi.

Coconuts

Coconuts are found on a number of the tropical islands. They grow wild and are usually found in abundance. Natives on the islands figured out a number of different ways to use the coconut. Coconut meat can be eaten plain or can be used to garnish dishes. Many use coconut meat in desserts such as cookies or cakes. Coconut milk has saved more than one starving lost person in the islands. It is extremely nutritious and is one of the few things that people can drink when in a foreign country without having to worry about getting any parasites. Coconut milk is used in a number of different dishes on the island. It is sometimes used to sweeten a stew or soup, and other times is used to marinate a meat in. Coconut milk has a way of softening up a piece of meat that not many marinades do.

Other Dishes

Many of the islands in Oceana that are close to Asia use rice and noodles, just as the Asian culture does. The starches are a staple in the diet, served with almost every meal. One dish that is popular is called nasi goreng. Nasi goreng is created when fried rice is mixed with other items. Sometimes the leftovers from the night before are thrown into the dish and it is served for breakfast. Chicken is also cooked frequently on the islands. Some islands spice the chicken up and grill it, while others make a type of chicken soup out of it. Many of the island chickens are allowed to run wild and are skinnier and have more muscles because of it.

Wine is not a very complex drink, considering the basic idea of wine. It is made from grapes that have been turned into juice. The juice is allowed to ferment and the result is wine. That's it! But, it is this fermentation process that is critical in wine-making, this itself decides most palate properties of the wine. Not that the quality of grapes is irrelevant, though. There are a number of different varieties and types of wine, beginning with the basic white and red. People around the world are beginning to love wine. They are enjoying it, in fact, so much that many are touring the world just to taste brands specific to some parts of the world.

Wine Tour

A wine tour is when a traveler goes to specifi destinations in order to view wine being made or taste a variety of different wines. Some are lucky enough to have vineyards a short distance away, but others need to trave thousands of miles in order to taste that elusive glass of wine that they have been searching for. Not that they would mind!

The difference in wines comes in the fermenting process and in the grapes. There are dozens of types of grapes, and each grape ferments a little differently than any other. When more than two grapes are added together, another type of wine is formed. This means that there are dozens of different subtle nuances in the smell, look, and flavor of the wine.

Chapter 3

Food Festivals

A food festival is a festival, usually held annually, that uses food, often produce, as its central theme. "These festivals have always been a means of uniting communities through celebrations of harvests and giving thanks for a plentiful growing season. They can be traced back thousands of years to celebrating the arrival of harvest time, the autumnal equinox, and the honoring of earth gods." The largest one in the United States (and the world) is the Taste of Chicago held in Chicago, Illinois.

FOOD FESTIVALS IN THE U.S.

There are several Florida food festivals and New Jersey food festivals.

Other festivals include the Gilroy Garlic Festival in Gilroy, California; Brentwood Cornfest in Brentwood, California; Mushroom Festivals in various locales; the Castroville Artichoke Festival, in Castroville, California; the Stockton Asparagus Festival, in Stockton, California; the Posen Potato Festival, in Posen, Michigan; the Norwalk Oyster Festival, in Norwalk, Connecticut, and the Howell Melon Festival in Howell, Michigan, known for electing the Howell Melon Queen.

Increasingly, vegetarian food festivals are becoming some of the largest food celebrations in the country, including Vegfest in Salt Lake City, Utah, Seattle,

Washington and San Francisco, California. Here at the office we love a bit of foodie gossip and are forever ploughing through interesting food and recipes sites to keep ourselves entertained (whilst working incredibly hard putting together a fantastic day for all you food fanatics out there as well obviously!). Anyway we feel like there is so much going on all of the time that we just simply HAVE to share it with you all so here it is! It's not going to be rocket science and we aren't going to be solving the big bang theory it's going to do exactly what it says on the tin so welcome to the Ponderings of a Foodie! I also want to let you know that there is no paying to appear on this page if we find a product and we love it we will tell you all about it!!

Did you eat at the Nestlé Toque d'Or Restaurant at this year's BBC Summer Good Food Show

If you ate in the Restaurant on Friday, then you'll have experienced the food from the 2010 champions from University College Birmingham! Join us in congratulating this team of up and coming chefs and restauratuers.

And here's the winning menu from this spectacular final of the Nestlé Toque d'Or Competition:

If that whet's your appetite, remember to check back here for details of how to book your place in next year's competition restaurant!

It is our new favourite programme here in the office - Taking the wonderful Roland and Miranda and their absolutely divine looking burgers along with the Singh Family and their super hot chilli sauce and making their dreams come true! We have had Muddy Boots and Mr Singh's at MasterChef Live and the BBC Good Food Show Birmingham before and we have always loved their products!! They will all be at the BBC Summer Good Food Show at the NEC in June so come and meet the people behind these wonderful products! We are always looking for exciting and interesting ways to keep up with the latest foodie trends and ideas and we think we have the perfect way to do this throughout May!! 30 Days of Food and Drink is packed full of recipe ideas, fantastic giveaways, foodie events and offers throughout the whole of May! They will send you a frequent newsletter to let you know what's going on and what you really can't miss! We are just too excited for words here in the organisers office that after six weeks of heats, a week of gruelling semi-finals and a week of finals, Dhruv Baker was awarded his trophy by judges: restaurateur John Torode and food writer and ingredients expert, Gregg Wallace.

Dhruv Baker said: "I had always secretly hoped to win MasterChef but not until the finals did I actually allow myself to believe I could actually win. It's mind blowing!

John Torode said: "The guy has a talent that very few people will ever have, and that is to cook the most amazing fusion food that I've ever tasted."

Gregg Wallace said: "Dhruv, I've got to say, is probably one of the most amazing talents I've ever seen. He has the palate of an angel."

Throughout the final week Dhruv, alongside other finalists Alex Rushmer and Tim Kinnaird, had to demonstrate his creativity, skill and determination as the finalists undertook serious challenges.

These included; travelling to the Rajasthan desert in India for a gruelling three-day challenge in 100-degree heat including cooking for a Maharajah and his family in a Palace atop the hills of Jodhpur, for the first time ever, running their own restaurant for the evening for paying customers with their own food on the menu and with John Torode manning the pass, and finally the greatest challenge ever to be set on MasterChef - cooking for one of the world's greatest living chefs, the legendary Alain Ducasse, and five of his protégée's who between them hold an incredible 30 Michelin stars.

The final task was to prepare a three course meal for judges John Torode and Gregg Wallace. Dhruv's winning menu consisted of a starter of Saffron and Ginger Poached Lobster Tail with Celeriac Puree on Blanched Fennel with a Burnoisette Foam, a main of Venison with a Potato, Brunoise and Fenugreek Crust, Sugar Glazed Carrots on a Carrot and Cumin Puree, Confit Chestnuts and a Venison

Jus, and a Trio of Desserts consisting of: Poached Pear in Sauterne and Star Anise, Massala Chi Ice-cream, and a Chocolate Truffle with a Pistachio Topping.

Dhruv, will be appearing at the MasterChef Experience at the Summer Good Food Show in Birmingham on 16th - 20th June and we cannot wait to meet him there! He said: "Having spent my university career in Birmingham and also having family there means it's a home away from home. I'm so excited to be able to take part in the MasterChef Experience in Birmingham in June. I can't believe after finishing the competition I'm going to face judges John Torode and Gregg Wallace again - but I'm very much looking forward to it."

Don't forget if you guys want to have a little taster of what Dhruv and all of the other contestants went through you can take part in the Invention Test at the Show - For more information click here.

19March

If you love eggs then this will is going to be the greatest news for you! Waitrose have started selling Ostrich Eggs!! Is that the biggest boiled egg you have ever seen!!!

At £15.99 per egg they aren't the cheapest you will ever find - however 1 egg will make 32 souffles or 100 meringues so if you use them correctly they could definately be value for money!

The Daily Mail reports:

"They work very well as omelettes," said a spokesman. "Quite big ones." Waitrose egg buyer Frances Westerman added: "The ostrich egg is a real show-stopper, in terms of looks and taste.

"Our customers like experimenting with new foodie ideas. We've seen growing popularity of duck, pheasant and goose eggs. Now it's the turn of the ostrich to take off."

The Clarence Court Ostrich Eggs, from a Lincolnshire farm, cost £15.99 each and are laid by freerange birds kept in small colonies.

When presented with one, leading chef Rowley Leigh of Le Cafe Anglais in Bayswater, West London, opted to scramble it.

But his first conundrum to crack was how to get into it because the shell is so thick. Mr Leigh resorted to hammering a roasting spike into the top and bottom and blowing out the contents into a bowl.

For good measure, he scored the top of the egg with a knife and cut it off with scissors to drain the last drops. Having scrambled the content she put them back in the shell to serve.

"We are not talking about the realms of practicalities here, we are talking about fun," he said.

"It tastes very much like a normal egg. It would go nicely with caviar. It tastes very creamy and rich but I wouldn't want to eat a lot of it."

Alwyn Williams - a former Welsh Guardsman is planning on sailing across to the isle of man - nothing exciting about that I hear you cry - untill you realise he is planning to do it IN A PUMPKIN!

It is indeed - this pumpkin will weigh in at a minimum of 7000lbs and measure 14 feet in circumference, powered by an outboard motor for the 45 mile trip!

Alwyn is not in this alone however he comes from a line of horticultural stars - his father is Medwyn Williams - 10 times gold medal winner at the Chelsea Flower Show - so he is sure to be a great help!

The scariest part of all...

Alwyn hasn't even sown the pumpkin yet! - He is planning to sow at the beginning of April hoping to get a growth rate of 35lbs a day between July and August.

It's all for a good cause though - Alwyn will be doing this to raise money for Help For Heroes.

Fantastic tea!!

Everyone knows the first thing one looks for in the morning is that cup of tea (well for some it's coffee but I am definately a tea girl!). Katy (Section Manager for the Producers' Village - remember she found the Graze boxes!!) has found the most fantastic company which is sure to bring style and panache to your morning cuppa! The company is called Tea Forte and not only do they have the most fantastic range of teas from Coco Truffle to Orchid Vanilla

but they also have the most fantastic range of Cocktail Blends: Make a fabulous Mojito with their Lemongrass Mint or my favourite is the Lavendar Citrus which can be used to "Infuse the natural flavours of white tea and lavender into Martinis, Cosmopolitans or your own inspired creations." WOW!!!! Tea all of a sudden got seriously interesting - if it helps make a better Cosmo then really what more do you need!!

Its all about Rhubarb!!!!

The news seems to be going a bit rhubarb crazy recently and we are loving the fact that Forced Rhubarb has now joined the ranks of Champagne and Parma ham on a list for Europe's specially protected food and drink!

The Yorkshire post said:

'It means only companies who produce the vegetable - in this case in the so-called "rhubarb triangle" between Bradford, Wakefield and Leeds - can use the name, guaranteeing the product is authentic and preventing imitation throughout Europe.'

Rhubarb is in season at the moment and BBC Good Food website has some great recipes for you but our favourite is definately James Martins Rhubarb, ginger, whisky and custard crumble tart with rhubarb compote - YUM!!!

Here it is for you - If you give it a go then do let us know what you think!!

Ingredients

For the tart

500g/1lb 2oz sweet pastry, rolled out to 5mm/¼in thickness

1.5kg/3lb 4oz rhubarb, cut into 5cm/2in lengths

3-4 tbsp caster sugar

4 tbsp whisky

3 pieces stem ginger, finely chopped

For the custard

150ml/5fl oz double cream

150ml/5fl oz whole milk

3 free-range eggs

2 free-range egg yolks

75g/3oz caster sugar

For the crumble topping

75g/3oz butter

150g/5oz plain flour

75g/3oz demerara sugar

Method

1. Preheat the oven to 180C/365F/Gas 4.
2. Place the rolled-out pastry into a deep loose-bottomed tart case and press the pastry into the sides. Place into the fridge to chill for 30 minutes, then remove and line the pastry case with baking parchment. Fill the tart case with rice or baking beans and place onto a baking sheet.
3. Place into the oven to bake blind for 15 minutes, then remove the rice or baking beans and baking parchment and return the tart case to the oven. Bake for a further 10-12 minutes, or until golden-brown and cooked.
4. Meanwhile, place the rhubarb onto a baking tray and cover with the sugar, to taste, whisky and ginger. Transfer to the oven to roast for 15 minutes, or until the rhubarb is tender.
5. For the custard, place the cream and milk into a pan and bring to the boil.
6. Place the eggs, egg yolks and sugar into a bowl and whisk to combine.

7. Pour the hot milk and cream mixture over the eggs mixture and whisk well to combine.
8. Return the custard to the pan over a low heat and bring to a gentle simmer, stirring constantly, until the custard has thickened.
9. For the crumble topping, place the butter and flour into a bowl and rub together with your fingers to form a breadcrumb-like mixture.
10. Add the sugar and mix to combine.
11. Pour the crumble mixture onto a baking tray and place into the oven to bake for 15 minutes, or until golden-brown. Remove from the oven and stir the crumble topping to break it up into pieces.
12. To assemble the crumble, place three-quarters of the rhubarb into the tart case, packing the rhubarb as densely as possible.
13. Pour the custard over the top, then transfer to the oven to bake for 15 minutes, or until the custard has just set.
14. Remove from the oven and sprinkle the custard with the crumble topping.
15. Place the remaining rhubarb into a small food processor and blend to a purée.
16. To serve, place a slice of tart onto each plate and serve with a spoonful of the rhubarb compote alongside.

FOOD OR GASTRONOMIC TOURISM AND RURAL DEVELOPMENT

During the 20th Century, industrialisation began to threaten artisan producers and many abandoned their traditional techniques. But in the past two decades, there has been a resurgence in demand for quality products made by time-honoured methods.

Gastronomy is one of the elements incorporated in a new concept of cultural heritage and cultural tourism, driven by growing trends of a well-being lifestyle, authenticity, environmental protection and the need to have a high-quality experience. Tourists increasingly want foods which emphasise the heritage and culture of a place, which assist the preservation of traditional forms of agriculture and cultural heritage.

Gastronomy, as a tourist resource, is appreciated not only for its own sake, but also for its ability to generate rural development. Gastronomic tourism is helping to increase rural revenue sources and improve income levels and employment of local labour (especially women).

Food also holds a key place in the "think globally, act locally" debate. Some buyers are keen to support local businesses, or protect the environment by avoiding foods which have been transported iong distances.

What are the Trends Driving Food tourism

Trend 1: Trading up

All across world, growing affluence of the populations has a profound impact on consumer spending. Consumers spend a higher proportion of their income on prepared food, gourmet products, eating out and food items with some form of health or ethical benefits. For discretionary purchases, consumers have traded up where the product is aspiration or traded down when the product is only function.

Trend 2: Demographics and Household Change

An ageing population and changing life styles have driven demand for increased eating out and food tourism opportunities. Groups that provide growing markets for food tourism are summarised in the table below.

Groups that provide growing markets for food tourism

DINKS: Double Income No Kids.

SINKS: Single Income No Kids.

Both Dinks and Sinks: younger people, between 25 and 35 years of age, no children, affluent.

Empty Nesters: parents whose children have flown the family nest. Between 45 and 55 of age, well educated, high disposable income.

Boomers: members of the baby boom generation in the 1950s.

Divorcees: searching for new partners and subsequently will take prospective partners out for dinner and away for romantic weekends.

Trend 3: Rejection of 'MacDonaldisation'

Tourists have increasingly rejected the industrial 'fordist' model of low cost mass production of food, searching out local, fresh and good quality cuisine that reflects the authenticity of the destination. The end of the 'MacDonaldisation' of food culture has seen Starbucks fail in Australia as the brand is perceived as bland and lacking individuality.

Trend 4: Growth of the Multi-Cultured Consumer

Multiculturalism has become an everyday concept in the daily life of the consumer, driven by immigration, globalisation, the internet, the expansion in specialist and minority TV channels and the relentless growth in international tourism. What were once exotic foods have become foods of first choice and today curry is the United Kingdom's favourite dish.

Trend 5: The Role of the Celebrity Chef and Media

The emergence of the niche food programmes, TV channels and magazines means the food celebrity and expert has been created. The celebrity chef shapes tourism products in a way that is often referred to as the 'Delia effect' after the media chef Delia Smith, whose 1998 television programme 'How to Cook' resulted in an extra 1.3 million eggs being sold in Britain each day of the series. The phenomena of Gordon Ramsey with 'Hells Kitchen' and the 'F word' or Jamie

Oliver's campaign for good wholesome school dinners all drives our interest in good quality food.

Malaysian food is not one particular kind of food but a unique culinary spectrum originating from Malaysia's multi-ethnic population that has melded together sampling tastes, ingredients and cooking methods from each other.

Malaysians relish and celebrate their diverse food choices. It is not uncommon to drive for hours to eat a really good bowl of noodles. As you can imagine, eatery standards are very competitive all over the country.

Each state in Malaysia has something different to offer in terms of culinary delights. Kuala Lumpur has the most diverse offering of foods from all over the world. Indulge in gourmet fusion cuisine created by talented chefs in designer restaurants, or sample an endless amount of goodies found practically bursting out of malls, store fronts and side-street hawker stalls.

Melaka is also home to delicious Baba Nyonya food, much of it served in quaint cafes in historical shophouses. Penang is hawker stall haven, where the most delicious food requires you to wait for al fresco tables and costs as little as RM3.50 per dish. Ipoh receives many day trippers who come only to savour local favourites.

Kelantan is the cradle of Malay culture and serves exotic Malay food rich in flavour and colour. When trying to decide on what stall or restaurant to visit, the rule of thumb is that the most popular place, especially among the locals, is normally the best.

This multi-cultural array of food has now come to be known all over the world as Malaysian Food. For gastronomic adventures fit for kings, the time is now, the place is Malaysia.

Renowned as the culinary capital of Asia, Hong Kong boasts more than 11,000 restaurants, many of them clustered in defined food districts. Apart from enjoying the best Cantonese and regional Chinese food, visitors can sample a full choice of authentic Asian cuisines and Western fare. Local must-try dishes are dim sum and fresh seafood, with some of the top examples found in Best of the Best award-winning restaurants.

HIGHLIGHTS

Dim Sum

Dim sum is a wide range of delightful Chinese snacks served in bamboo baskets accompanied by Chinese tea. Having dim sum in Hong Kong is a unique experience you shouldn't miss.

Seafood

For a distinctive culinary experience, try the fresh seafood. The freshness is guaranteed as you can select live fish from tanks at the restaurant. Whether you like steamed, fried or grilled seafood, try it cooked Hong Kong-style!

Quality Tourism Services (QTS) Scheme

The QTS Scheme makes it easy for you to find restaurants that you can trust. Just look for the QTS sign displayed prominently by restaurants that have qualified for this exclusive award.

Gastro-tourism is a growing international trend shaping our choice of holiday and while Italy and France are often thought of as the traditional European food destinations, other countries are waking up to the opportunity to spice up their own tourist trade.

Finland is well placed to raise its profile in the industry and according to Statistics Finland, a national agency, people are travelling to the country in ever-growing numbers. The number of overnight stays by foreign tourists was up more than 10 per cent on the previous year and Finland is proving increasingly popular with Russian tourists in particular. Visitors from the Baltic States, Great Britain and China are also making a strong contribution.

Appealing to Our Emotions

One of the reasons for the growing popularity of gastro-tourism is our emotional connection with food. "Food leaves a lasting impression on our senses and gives you a real feel for a region's culture and history. Exotic local flavours linger long in the memory," says Eeva Blomqvist from Finfood - Finnish Food Information.

"Local, seasonal, genuine and 'small is beautiful' are important themes. The culture, origins and traditions linked to food add yet another dimension to the eating experience," says Ms Blomqvist who has studied food tourism.

Food Tourists Spoilt for Choice

As well as dining at restaurants, food tourism can often take in visits to farms and food and drink festivals, and benefit from themed package tours and trips.

"In England you can find for example a tour focusing on tea, wine or even sausages, while in Scotland you can follow the Whisky Route," Eeva explains. And then there's a lobster safari in Sweden. Finnish food tourism promotions include for instance the Skärgårdssmak concept that introduces the treasures of the famous southern Archipelago.

Getting a Taste of Real Food in the Countryside

According to Vesa Heikkinen, Research Director of Tourism Studies at the University of Lapland, a leading trend in Finnish gastro-tourism is to seek out unique products courtesy of rural ventures, and people come a long way to sample such treats. Genuine tastes and idyllic milieus attract tourists who are simply fed up with amusement parks.

"A food tourist attraction doesn't necessarily have to offer a ten-course meal. Even a small company can succeed with a product that's not available in shopping centres," Dr Heikkinen suggests.

Many people would agree that one of the finest aspects of traveling is dining at local restaurants. But, food tourism is on the move to something much bigger-the ultimate gourmet experience, and the only way you can truly learn about a cuisine-is to take an international cooking class in its country of origin.

When you travel to Parma, Italy, you are actually taking a journey into centuries-old Italian culinary history. Next, when you cook food using the ingredients from that specific local, such as the only true Parmigiano Reggiano in the world (an aged Parmesan cheese) named after the province of Parma where it is produced, that is when food meets with art and the celebration of a country.

Discover Spain when harvesting Spanish olives, then making them into olive oil. Or, traveling to the home of Spain's most popular sheep's milk cheese "Manchego" made from the milk of sheep grazing on the plains of La Mancha, or sipping regional wines such as the famed sherries from Jerez and Montilla.

Imagine: after a hunt for rare black truffles in France and then a shopping excursion at a Parisian open-air market, learning traditional French culinary techniques and preparing your treasure in a Provençal farmhouse kitchen. Or, serving-up genuine Creole and Cajun recipes in New Orleans and then dining on the feast with Dixieland jazz in the background.

HONG KONG FOOD

Looking for a Tour Contact Us

Hong Kong is the culinary capital of Asia. A gastronomical tour of Asia without a visit to Hong Kong would be incomplete. Hong Kong is a placc which offers superb cuisine from around the world and an infinite choice of restaurants.

Here is concise information about food recipe in Hongkong:

Hong Kong Hits!

If you are on a tour of Hong Kong, never fail to bite into Dim Sum, the tasty collection of delicacies served in bamboo steamers, or crisp Peking Duck carved at your table. Be sure to try Jumbo Restaurant, counted among the world's most luxurious floating restaurant. And Hong Kong also holds Ocean City Restaurant and Night Club, which seats more than 4800 people.

Dim Sum

Dim Sum is the most famous in the long list of dishes in a Hongkong meal. Impressively shaped, bite-size portions of dumplings with lightly seasoned fillings of meat and seafish, fluffy buns with various fillings and glutinous rice - all deliciously steamed - just ignite the tastebuds.

Treat your taste buds

New Zealand's Food and Wine Festivals bring together a comprehensive selection of gourmet delicacies from different regions, served up in beautiful scenic settings, with a splash of world class wine and a sprinkling of New Zealand's best live entertainment.

"Festivals" are the perfect way to sample the many and varied culinary and geographical delights New Zealand has to offer. And from November to February, you can take it all in on a deliciously long, hot summer day.

Toast Martinborough

Sunday 21st of November 2010

Toast Martinborough celebrates the release of the new vintage of wines and is centred around the charming Martinborough Wine Village. From there it's just an easy stroll (or catch the free Shuttle bus) to any of the eleven boutique vineyards dotted around the picturesque countryside, each with its own distinctive style and entertainment. Move on at your leisure, sampling delights for all the senses!

Tickets go on sale at 9am on 6th October 2010 at Ticketek, but be in quick, they sell out very fast!

Tauranga Moana Seafood Festival

Saturday 27th November 2010

This is your chance to savour some of New Zealand's finest seafood delicacies. And it's an event the whole family can enjoy.

Situated along the waterfront, the Tauranga Moana Seafood Festival is the perfect excuse to simply sit back, relax and let the musical entertainment wash over you. Or, get involved and cheer on the competitors in the fish filleting and mussel opening competitions. There's Kapa Haka, harbour cruises and cooking demonstrations, while the children (or simply young at heart!) are also spoilt for choice with a bouncy slide, treasure hunt and monster Sandcastle competition.

Then of course, there's the SEAFOOD! Crayfish, whitebait, paua fritters, seafood chowder and salmon kebabs... the mouth-watering list goes on and on.

Rhythm and Vines

Wednesday 29th to Friday 31st December 2010

Rather than treating your taste buds, Rhythm and Vines is an audio visual feast! And it's the perfect way to see in the New Year. Gisborne is, after-all, the first place in the world to see the sun rise on 2011. Set amongst the vines and rolling hills of Waiohika Estate, this is Party Central.

Now in its eighth year, Rhythm and Vines will thrill and amaze, as well as entertain you. With its themed stages, the latest world class audio systems, dazzling light shows, fireworks and a lavish programme of bands and musicians including N*E*R*D, Justice DJ, Shihad, Chromeo and Boys Noize, to name just a few. But the entertainment doesn't stop there.... add the famous R&V waterslide , the ever popular forest stage, costumed circus performers and a whole heap of wonderful surprises... and you have a New Year's Eve you'll never forget!

Rhythm and Vines accommodation options also vary wildly, from camping on-site to luxury alternatives.

Harvest Hawke's Bay

Saturday 29th January 2011

The beautiful Hawke's Bay region is famous for its world-class wine and food making it a natural choice as a location to celebrate everything gourmet.

Harvest Hawke's Bay showcases some of the best this region has to offer, with more than 40 top wineries and boutique food producers gathered at the new Roy's Hill venue. Unlike other Festivals, Harvest Hawke's Bay brings its exhibitors together in one purpose-built facility, overlooking the renowned Gimblett Gravels wine growing area, and surrounded by stunning vineyard and mountain views.

As well as enlightening your palate, Harvest Hawke's Bay can enlighten your mind. Workshops run throughout the day offering classes from matching wine and food, to the art of cooking seafood.

And of course it wouldn't be a kiwi Wine and Food Festival without superb live entertainment from some of New Zealand's top performers.

Auckland Seafood Festival

Auckland also has a piece of the Festival pie with a focus on fun at the vibrant 3 day Auckland Seafood Festival. On offer are a range of delicious gourmet New Zealand seafood, wine sampling from some of Auckland's finest vineyards and great family entertainment throughout the weekend, including surfcasting competitions and cooking demon-strations.

From noon to 7pm, Auckland's Viaduct Harbour comes alive with the vibrant Festival atmosphere. The Auckland Seafood Festival is for seafood lovers, wine and beer connoisseurs alike!

Fish for further details here - tickets are not on sale yet.

Marlborough Wine Festival

The Marlborough Wine Festival is New Zealand's longest running wine festival.

Set in the heart of one of Marlborough's oldest and most beautiful vineyards, Montana Brancott Estate, the Marlborough Wine Festival is New Zealand's longest running wine festival.

Marlborough's proud reputation for producing world class wines will be showcased with around 60 wineries and 30 local producers offering their most delicious gourmet delights.

With all the talented winemakers about you're sure to learn a thing or two at the 'Wine Tutorials' or put your best foot forward and enter the 'Fashion in the Vines' competition for the best dressed man and woman.

But if that sounds far too strenuous, simply sit back and enjoy the sumptuous wine and food, great entertainment and glorious setting!

The Marlborough Wine Festival is New Zealand's longest running and most successful wine festival. Come and sample a unique selection of Marlborough wines along with some delicious local produce and gourmet cuisine. The festival has something for everyone including wine tutorials with the regions' leading winemakers and viticulturists, Thomas's Fashion in the Vines competition, the Food and wine matching competition and fantastic entertainment from some of New Zealand's leading performers.

Ghana

Many festivals include thrilling durbars of chiefs, when tribal leaders and Queen Mothers process in decorated palanquins, shaded by the traditional umbrellas, and supported by drummers and warriors discharging ancient muskets. The dates of many festivals are determined by the traditional calendars, often decided close to the event.

AKWASIDEE FESTIVAL - FESTIVAL OF THE KINGS

7 days : Join paramount, divisional and sub chiefs to pay homage to Otumfuo Osei Tutu II, King of the powerful Asanteman Kingdom during the colourful spectacular that is the Akwasidee festival which is celebrated every 42 days (every sixth Sunday).Click to view full itinerary

Aboakyir Festival - May Each Year

This Festival is celebrated by the people of Simpa or Winneba in the Central Region of Ghana. The festival is a celebration to mark the migration of these people from the ancient Western Sudan Empire where they were led by 2 brothers and a god called Otu. Upon consulting their god, they were instructed by their traditional priest or mediator between the people and the god to sacrifice a young member of the Royal family every year to their god.

Panafest

Panafest is a biennial festival of African dance, music and other performing arts that is held every two years in Ghana.

A cultural event dedicated to the enhancement of the ideals of Pan-Africanism and the development of the African continent. It is organized biennially for Africans and people of Africa descent as well as all persons committed to the well being of Africans on continent and in the diaspora. The essential thrust of PANAFEST is to enhance DEVELOPMENT.

The Homowo Festival - August/September

The word "Homowo" actually means 'making fun of hunger.' Our traditional oral history describes a time long ago when the rains stopped and the sea closed its gates. A deadly famine spread throughout the southern Accra Plains, the home of the Ga people. When the harvest finally arrived and food became plentiful, the people were so happy that they celebrated with a festival that ridiculed hunger.

The Hogbetsotso Festival

This is celebrated on the first Saturday of November every year by the Anlo Ewes of the Volta Region of Ghana. The essential feature of this festival is a magnificent durbar of chiefs and citizens. Hogbetsotso, generally known as "the festival of the Exodus" is held annually to commemorate the escape of the Anlo Ewes from the tyrannical ruler of Notsie - Agokoli of Togo. The chiefs appear on the durbar grounds in their most charming royal regalia and sit in state to acknowledge and receive homage from their subjects. The entire ceremony is laced with non-stop soul-stirring drumming and dancing.

Ivory Coast

Bouake Carnival - towards end March- April

Another important event is the week long carnival in Bouaké each March, a festivity attracting thousands of visitors.

Fêtes des Masques (Festival of Masks) - November

One of Côte d'Ivoire's most famous festivals is the Fêtes des Masques (Festival of Masks), which takes place in the region of Man occurs in November. Numerous small villages in the region hold contests to determine the best dancers and to pay homage to forest spirits who are embodied in the elaborate masks.

Fête du Dipri - April

Held in Gomon, near Abidjan, this festival starts around midnight, when women and children sneak out of their huts and, naked, carry out nocturnal rites to exorcise the village of evil spells. Before sunrise the chief appears, drums pound and villagers go into trances. The frenzy continues until late afternoon of the next day.

MALI

Festival in the Desert (Festival-au-Desert)

This is truly a one-of-a-kind experience! Visit the festival yourself with this 14 day itinerary.

Billed as the "most remote music festival in the world" the Festival is a three-day Afro-pop powwow held by the Tuareg, the traditionally nomadic "blue people" of the Sahara. It's a tribe often feared for the banditry of its rebels and respected for the fact that it has never really been conquered. Combining traditional Tuareg music and dance, camel races, and competitions during the day, the Festival comes alive at night with modern Malian music, which is becoming popular the world over from incorporation into music as diverse as that of Robert Plant and Paul Simon. Although the centerpoint of this trip is the Festival in the Desert in Essakane, the itinerary also includes more well-known Mali attractions such as Dogon country, Djenne, and Timbuctu.

Festival on the NigerJan/Feb Segou

tradional malian musique and dance, a Forum with theme "development trough culture and tourism", a Fair with local art and food.

Fête des Masques - April

The Dogons are famous for their masks and during the five-day event many of them are used in ritual ceremonies that go back more than 1000 years. At each Sigui festival, a new ceremonial mask is carved especially for the occasion, then placed in the Tellem caves. Remnants of these masks going back hundreds of years have been found in the caves.

Crossing of the Cattle - December

The Cattle Crossing is the most important Fulani festival in Diafarabe. Every December, herders bring cattle from the grazing lands to the river at Diafarabe. Here everyone crosses the river. On the other side families are reunited for a few days, before they take the cattle to new pastures. The first day is the Promenade des Jeunes, when the unmarried men and women dress up to attract each other. There is also a competition to judge the fattest and best looked-after cattle, with useful prizes.

Nigeria

Durbar Festival - Oct

The Durbar festival is celebrated at the culmination of the two great Muslim festivals Id el Fitri and Id el Kabir. The festival gives a good idea of the past glories of the emirate before the influence of western culture.

EASTERN AFRICA

Kenya

International Camel Derby & Festival - August (TBC)

The Derby takes place at Maralal, Samburu District, centred at Yare Club & Camp, just four kilometres south of Maralal town on the Nyahururu road. . It is also a spectacular festival packed with a variety of events that draws visitors from all over the world. The Derby has been on the go since 1990, with entries from Australia, America, New Zealand, Canada, England, France, Spain, Japan, South Africa and beyond competing against the reigning Kenya champions in both the amateur and professional races. The route runs through semi-desert regions with varying levels of difficulty and camels (with or without handlers) are available to hire for those wishing to compete.

Nairobi International Book Fair

The emphasis is locally published books and magazines, but is now starting to attract the attention of publishers elsewhere in Africa and elsewhere overseas. Targets the publishing trade as well as the public. Up to 20,000 visitors, including schools groups. Provides a platform for the dynamic marketing and promotion service industry, and targets promotional book-signings, book-readings, book-launches and a comprehensive seminar programme.

The Schweppes East African Concours d' Elegance.

Nairobi Racecourse. The annual vehicle beauty contest organized by the Alfa Romeo Owners Club for all makes and types of cars, pick ups, station wagons and motorcycles.

Mombasa Carnival - November

The Mombasa carnival features parades and floats from every conceivable cultural, national and religious group in Kenya. There are two main parades which converge onto Moi Avenue which feature incredible floats, spectacular costumes and fantastic music.

Tanzania/Kenya

The Wildebeest Migration

The Wildebeest Migration in East Africa, also known as "The Great Migration" takes place between Tanzania's Serengeti National Park and Kenya's Masai Mara and is one of the greatest wildlife spectacles on the planet.

Thousands of wildebeest and zebra's migrate between the Serengeti and the Masai Mara, constantly driven by their search for fresh grazing. The massive herds are closely followed by predators (lion, hyena and cheetah), making the most of every opportunity to catch their next meal.

The precise timing of the annual wildebeest migration depends on the rains. It is a very unpredictable and spontaneous natural event, with calving season taking place in the Serengeti between January and mid-March. The wildebeest migration starts to head towards the Western Serengeti in May or June. The best time to see the migration is generally between June and August when the wildebeest congregate and prepare to cross the famous Grumeti River.

If you are in the Masai Mara you can expect the wildebeest to make their arrival as early as July, but they generally arrive between August & September and remain in the Masai Mara between October & November. Between the end of November and January the wildebeest gradually begin their migration from the Masai Mara back towards the Serengeti.

The Great Wildebeest Migration - Lodge Safari

11 days: This safari allows you to witness the very best of Tanzania. You will revel in all the wildlife viewing opportunities on the fabled plains of the Serengeti, around Lake Manyara, Tarangire & Ngorongoro. Spend four nights at the lodge in Serengeti and spend the days on game drives tracing the direction of the wildebeests migration. This itinerary can be customised to suit you. Click to view full itinerary

UGANDA

Bayimba International Festival of Music and Arts - 17 - 19 September 2010

The Annual Bayimba International Festival of Music and Arts - a vibrant platform to celebrate the power of Music and Arts in Uganda.

ZANZIBAR

Sauti za Busara music festival 9 - 13 February 2011

Features a rich variety of African music from the region with more than four hundred musicians participating over five days in historic Stone Town.

Festival of the Dhow Countries July

East Africa's largest cultural event, takes place in Zanzibar in magnificent, historical venues along the waterfront of Stone Town. The festival celebrates the unique cultural heritage of the "Dhow" countries: the African continent and the Indian Ocean region and their global Diaspora.

Mwakakogwa Festival - July/August

A traditional festival to celebrate the local New Year. It is mainly practiced in the Southern Unguja, particularly in Makunduchi. Originating from Persia and brought here by early, Immigrants, Mwakakogwa is marked by sacrifices, dances, and the actual field fighting. In addition to the tourists from abroad, it draws participants from the whole of East Africa.

NORTHERN AFRICA

Sahara Marathon - February

Travel to North Africa and live and run in this most difficult yet breathtaking place on earth-The Sahara Desert.

Telefónica-Dakar Rally - Dates tbc

Tits rich, eventful and adventurous past, its adaptability to its time, and to the men and women of its time, the Dakar has become a major highlight of the sporting calendar. Crossing of Portugal, Spain, Morocco, Mauritania, Mali, Guinea and Senegal.

Egypt

Egyptian Maraton Luxor

The Marathon is an international event with over 36 nationalities participating and it is the only A I M S (Association of international Marathons and Road Races) certified Marathon in the country.

Pharaonic Race - CairoNovember

100Kms : The route of the race will take you first to sites of Sakkara , the ancient necropolis of Memphis, Egypt's earliest capital. The third highlight will be the magnificent area of Dahshure , where the bent and the red Pyramids of King Snefru can be admired.

Abu Simbel Festival - Twice every year, 22nd February and 22nd October)

Abu Simbel is located in the heart of Nubia and is accessible by road or air from Aswan. The most remarkable feature of the site is that the temple is precisely oriented so that twice every year, on 22 February and 22 October, the first rays of the morning sun shine down the entire length of the temple-cave to illuminate the back wall of the innermost shrine and the statues of the four gods seated.

Ramses II, in a fit of precision and despotic architectural egotism, carefully angled his temple at Abu Simbel so that the inner sanctum would light up twice a year: once on the anniversary of his rise to the throne, and once on his birthday. The combination of human endeavour and natural phenomena provides what must be one of the most spectacular sights in the world.

South Sinai Camel Festival - May

This festival gives all travelers a chance to change their opinion regarding camels being slow plodders. The most speediest and bumpiest racing of all, takes place at Sharm El-Sheikh.

Cairo Film Festival

With its ancient history, and vast motion picture industry, Egypt became the cultural capital of the Arab world. Egypt's cinema's influence on the Arabs is as profound as that of the American cinema on the rest of the world. That why Cairo is known to be "Hollywood" of the Middle East.

ETHIOPIA

Ethiopia Religious Festival Tour

Ethiopia Historic Route tour is also designed in such a way to coincides with the colorful Festivals of Meskal,

Timkat, Christmas or Axum Tsion. You will enjoy beauty of Ethiopia religious festival celebrations.

Ethiopia Two major Festivals: Christmas and Timket

The best time to make a holiday to Ethiopia is on the date of its festivals. Book this special tour to attend the celebration of the two major festivals- Christmas in Lalibela and Timket in Addis Ababa. The tour also includes a visit of Ethiopia Historic Route Tigray Rock Churches and Simien Mountain National park.

Ethiopia Timket Festival: Celebrating in Lalibela

The main Highlights of this Ethiopia tour is to visit the celebration of Ethiopian Epiphany- Timket, on 19 January in Lalibela. Lalibela is one of the Holy towns in the country; Timket festival is celebrated so colorfully and differently. It is the best place to attend Timket festival in Ethiopia. The tour also includes a visit of Ethiopia Historic Route.

Historic Route Simien Mountains & Hidar Tsion Festival - Ethiopia travel to the major historical and cultural tourist attractions to visit world heritage sites in Gondar, Lalibela, Axum, Harer & Simien Mountains with visit of Hidar Tsion Festival in Axum.

Historic Route Rift Valley Lakes & Meskel Festival

Ethiopia Tour to explore Monasteries on Lake Tana Castle of Gondar Rock churches in Lalibela Stles of Axum Simien Mountain National Park Harer and attend Meskel Festival celebration in Addis Ababa.

Omo Valley Bahir Dar Gonadr Axum & Ethiopian Christmas in Lalibela

Travel to the North Great Historic Route Ethiopia and South Rift/ Omo Valley with a visit of the religious celebration of Ethiopian Christmas.

Timkat/Epiphany - January

Timket, or the Feast of the Epiphany, is celebrated in the January of each year. The 3-day event commemorates the baptism of Christ and is one of the most colourful Ethiopian festivals. The night before the Timket, priests take the Tabot (which symbolises the Ark of the Covenant, containing the Ten Commandments) from each church to a tent at a consecrated pool or stream. There is frenetic activity, including the ringing of bells, blowing of trumpets and the burning of incense. In Addis Ababa, tents are pitched at Jan Meda, to the northeast of the city centre. At 02h00, mass is celebrated, attended by crowds of people carrying lighted oil lamps. At dawn, the priest uses a ceremonial cross to extinguish a candle burning on a pole in a nearby river. Inevitably, some of the congregation leap into the river. The Tabots are then taken back to the churches in procession, accompanied by horsemen, while the festivities continue.

Morocco

There are a couple of big annual events that help visitors unravel the mysteries of Morocco. Feasts are organized during all seasons, celebrating various local traditions. Festivals are consecrated to the arts and to the popular traditions. "Moussems" are important gathering to pay homage to a special personalities

Moroccan Moroccan Sacred Fez Music Festival & Tour : Artists from around the world flock to Morocco's spiritual capital during the annual Fez Sacred Music Festival. The event features performances in a variety of styles, ranging from local Sufi chants to haunting gypsy songs from Spain - a romantic setting for a fine selection of devotional music.

To satisfy even the most demanding customer, organizers add annual spectaculars to each year's program. This has included Whirling Dervishes from Iran. There are also concerts on the Bab Boujloud Square, children's educational activities and the famous Sufi nights at Dar Tazi......and much more.

Marrakech Popular Arts Festival /Marrakech

For five days now, the bustling city of Marrakech manages to cram in even more popular sights and sounds than it boasts already during the Marrakech Popular Arts Festival. The El- Badi Palace in particular acts as the centre of events over the course of the festival.

Essaouira Gnaoua and World Music Festival / Essaouira

the bustling city celebration of the mysterious music of the Gnawas, the product of a mystic tradition with branches as widespread as Haitian voodoo and Brazilian Candomblé. A picturesque port painted in blue and white, Essaouira is the ideal resort that most travelers dream of when they think of North Africa: laid-back and yet vibrant, atmospheric and relaxing.

Live 1001 night in the Moroccan Sahara New Year

Spend New Years Eve 2010 in Morocco. As night falls, watch traditional folkloric dance and listen to the heady intoxicating beat of Berber drum music and song during the traditional pouring of mint tea. delight in a Moroccan feast. At the crest of the gathering, the sun sets on an old year, outlining the dunes in a complexity worthy of the future: vast and unpredictable as the tales of Sheherazad, and the 1001 nights to be lived before the sun rises on 2009.

SOUTHERN AFRICA

LESOTHO

Morija Arts & Cultural Festival - October

Each year on the first Thursday of October, the Festival is alive and kicking again. The main days of the Festival will be Friday through Sunday. During the four days of the Festival about 40 events will take place at 8 venues in Morija which cater for all tastes in music, dance, drama and film. At the main Arena, Thabeng Football Grounds, are also found arts & crafts displays and sales, as well as information booths and tents marketing a wide range of products, including food and drinks of different traditions. Concerts, Jazz, Famo, Gospel & Kwaito will highlight each day.The friendly & festive atmosphere of this Festival is unique and each visitor is highly welcomed .

Music and Food Festivals

The Ministry of Education organises drama and music festivals for primary and secondary schools where traditional dances and folk music is performed. This event is held at different levels usually during the second term of the academic year which falls between the months of May to July each year. The general public is invited. Other educational institutions like colleges and Universities are also involved.

The Ministry of Home Affairs and National Heritage, through its Department of Culture organises a Cultural Music Festival annually; whose patron is the Head of State. This is specifically for non-educational institutions like Government departments, parastatals, and local clubs. The event is held at each province every October and at national level for a week at the Kenyatta International Conference Centre usually in August. During the event, traditional dances, acrobatics, folk music, etc., are performed.

Winners make their presentations at State House to the President and become Kenya's cultural choir the whole of the year where they are invited during national holidays and functions to entertain the public.

During this cultural festival, traditional foods from different ethnic groups are exhibited. Besides these traditional food exhibitions, internationally recognised cuisine and food specialities are organised for food exhibitions by interested hotels whose restaurants specialise in that cuisine, and co-sponsored by key industry players; both private and public. These do not have regular timings but are determined by the hotels.

The Kenya Utalii College organizes annually in July a one-day food festival usually called the "Uhondo Africa". Different cuisines from different parts of the world are displayed together with Kenya's own dishes from different cultural backgrounds. Visitors are welcome to have a true taste of these.

The Dugong Festival and the Lamu Donkey Racing

Lamu is a wonderful old stone town with a distinctive Arab traditional architecture, curved doors, narrow streets, absence of vehicles, many mosques, fishermen, women dressed in black and wearing the bui bui and is rich in the Muslim culture. The town is in the North Coast region of Kenya and takes tourism seriously as this is the major source of income. Residents of this historical town hold a festival in May each year under the name of the "Lamu Dugong festival" and incorporate the famous donkey race. Donkeys are the sole means of transport in Lamu and are found in large numbers! The festival lasts a week and brings together people from all sectors including visiting tourists. The major theme of the festival is to create awareness to the residents and the public about the need to conserve the Dugong found near the islands (mythologically known as the mermaid), which is an endangered species.

Other activities during this festival include dhow racing, water sports, traditional dances, food exhibitions fashion and architectural displays.

Nairobi and Mombasa Carnivals

Each year, Kenya's major cities hold entertainment and music extravaganzas to celebrate the cities' birth. Members of the public are usually invited and visiting tourists too. The first one in October 1998 was incorporated with the celebration of 50 years of the Mombasa and Coast Tourism Association and over 7000 tourists joined. Entertainment, food, art and culture displays, fashion shows and other outdoor sports form a grater part of the fun filled day.

This years Mombasa Carnival will be held on 4th November 2000. The carnivals parade will start from Moi Avenue and from Fort Jesus a place that reminds one of the precious history of Kenya. It will proceed up to Mama Ngina Drive where there will be a lot of activities.

Art Festivals

The National Museums of Kenya hold annually an Art festival in Nairobi called the East African Art Festival. The event takes three days only and draws exhibitors from the whole of the East African region. Exhibitors display their art works, paintings, traditional artifacts and architectural designs among others. Related technical institutions and colleges around the country hold other art exhibitions, and your local safari operator can give the dates.

Festivals Around National Holidays

Just before Kenya's holidays several events take place to commemorate these important national days which includes screening of films, performing plays and skits, releasing songs, etc, all about these events. This is organized by the National Museums of Kenya in conjunction with the Department of Culture, Ministry of Home Affairs.

When's a bamboo tent not a bamboo tent When you're in Calcutta. For, in this city, a step into a luxurious bamboo edifice known locally as a pandal could well be your baptism to the festive side of the city. Pandals, in which the idols of deities are places and worshippers congregate, are a staple of Hindu festivals Kolkata, but the festive landscape of Calcutta isn't about which religion you belong to. Festivals are a great opportunity to meet people, soak in the culture of the city, pamper your taste buds, discover the cosmopolitan side to the city and, of course, give yourself up to religious fervor.

Rathyatra

Travel along with the Lord of Puri, Jagannath, as his chariot takes him to his midsummer vacation. Legend has it that Jagannath, a reincarnation of Lord Vishnu, goes on this vacation with his brother Balaram and sister Subhadra. Religious fervor runs high and the streets of Calcutta turn into a mélange of colors. Devotees take turns to pull gigantic chariots bearing idols of the three divinities through the narrow bylanes of the city.

Do check out the Rathyatra in Mahesh in the nearby Hooghly district - it's the oldest in the state. The Mahesh Rathyatra of 1875 is also special as it provided the inspiration for Radharani, a famous novel by Bengali poet and author Bankim Chandra Chatterjee.

Saraswati Puja

If you wake up to streets dotted with young girls in yellow saris, don't get an eye test. Just throw on your best Indian wear and hurry down to the roads for the festivities of Saraswati Puja. Dedicated to Saraswati, the goddess of learning, science, and the creative arts, this festival is all the way for students. The youngest girl in every Bengali family is decked in yellow on this day, and students flock to the pandals to pray for their academic success.

For an all-night festive experience, catch the celebration of the "Night of Shiva". Devotees meditate, pray, sing and recite hymns in praise of Lord Shiva and offer milk, curd, honey and glossy green leaves of the bel tree in worship. Celebrated in February-March, the festival is also a time for the devotees to observe fasts. The Shivratri celebrations in Tarakeshwar, in the neighboring Hooghly, are special and worth a visit.

Poila Baisakh

The first month of the Bengali calendar, Baishakh, marks the beginning of the crop cycle in Bengal. A lot of Bengali weddings are held in this month, and new businesses started. The first day of this month is called Poila Baisakh is celebrated as the Bengali new year. Chances are, if you step into a shop in Calcutta on this day, you'll be offered sweets and maybe the odd gift or two. Traders start the new year by inaugurating new accounting books.

Id-ul-Fitr

Id-ul-Fitr marks the end of the holy Islamic month of Ramzan. Take a walk down the path alongside the Maidan on this day and watch the young, middle-aged and old alike gathering here for their prayers, harkening to the call of the muezzin from the Shahid Minar.

Muharram

The solemnity of Muharram is best experienced by following an "Ashoura" procession in the city. Led by a snow-white horse, the procession of tazias and the devout wends its way through areas such as Metiabruz and Khiderpore.

Kali Puja

A festival to propitiate the dark goddess Kali, Kali Puja is held in the dark of a new moon night. With her blue-black skin, blood-smeared face, terrifying third eye, Kali wears little other than necklaces of snakes and skulls. In her four hands, she bears weapons and blessings for her followers. This is one festival that is seldom performed within a home, and is often marked by animal sacrifices.

Makar Sankranti

A festival that marks the winter solstice, the Makar Sankranti festival is marked by two melas or fairs, both held a little distance from Calcutta. The maidan in Kolkata, however, plays host to the hordes of faithfuls thronging to the three-day Ganga Sagar Mela held on Sagardwip to commemorate this festival. Even as the Ganga Sagar Mela winds down, bauls - a cult of minstrels - wend their way to nearby Bolpur for the Baul mela.

Lakshmi Puja

Durga Puja is closely followed by Lakshmi Puja - the festival honoring the goddess of wealth, peace and prosperity. Every home celebrates this festival as a chance to welcome the goddess of wealth to their homes. A day or two before the festival, the bazaars of Kolkata are choc-a-bloc with vendors selling idols of the gracious Lakshmi, seated on a lotus.

Durga Puja

For four days in September-October, Calcutta comes to a standstill as almost everyone in the city throngs its streets, visiting the pandals dressed in their festive best and fêting their taste buds with food from the stalls that spring up on the roadsides. Incense, drumbeats, chants, laughter, the sizzle and smell of food characterize this festival dedicated to Goddess Durga. Durga Puja is a chance to meet old friends, rub shoulders with the young and eligible, buy new clothes, walk the streets of the city till the wee hours of the morning, and, of course, admire the oeuvre of idol makers who craft beautiful idols of Durga, Lakshmi, Saraswati, Ganesh and Kartik out of bamboo, straw, jute, clay and paint.

Joydev Mela

Strictly speaking, the Joydev Mela is held at Kenduli, a small village near Tagore's Shantiniketan, and not in Calcutta. However, this fair-cum-festival held in the early half of January and commemorating the birth of the Bhakti cult poet Jaydev is a wonderful way to connect with rural India. For three days, Baul minstrels, spiritual shoppers and city slickers seeking a high flock to this festival and lose themselves to the trance-like magic of baul songs.

Bhai Phota

This is the day brothers and sisters put aside their family squabbles and celebrate their familial ties. Women maintain a fast through the morning and break it by applying a dab of sandalwood to their brothers' foreheads, praying for their safety and welfare and plying them with sweets. In turn they receive gifts from their brothers. Do wangle an invite to a Bengali house on this day if you can - it's a day when the kitchen turns out some of its best fare of the year!

Dol Purnima

A festival of spring, Dol Purnima is marked by people merrymaking on the streets, smearing each other with color, drinking milk laces with marijuana (locally called bhang) and ambushing unsuspecting passers-by with water balloons. Some of the celebrations can get pretty rowdy and some of the colors can get pretty artificial, so stay in your room if your skin's sensitive.

Vishwakarma Puja

If you're in Calcutta in September, and know someone in a factory, a workman or an artisan, spend the early morning of this festive day in their company. Dedicated to the God of Creation, Vishwakarma, the true spirit of the festival is seen in the homes of craftsmen and in industrial houses. Machines are oiled, cleaned and painted, and tools scrubbed and polished till they reflect the idol of the god, holding a hammer in his hand.

Christmas

For the best picture-postcard feel during Christmas, take a stroll down Park Street on Christmas Eve. Midnight mass at St Paul's Cathedral is a different experience altogether, as the entire cathedral is lit up by candles. If you're in the vicinity of the shopping are called New Market, also drop by at the celebrated Nahoum's for the best bakes and cakes of the season.

FOOD PROMOTIONS IN BANGALORE CITY

Special Wine Dinner at The Zaman - ISTA Hotel

The Ista Hotel, No 1/1,Swami Vivekananda Road, Ulsoor

Special Wine Food Festival is organized at Ista - a hotel that takes its inspiration from its name. Experience world class cuisine at Ista's two restaurants and one lounge bar, each with it's own distinctive character, attitude and style.

'Indian Classics' Food Promotion at Zaman Restaurant

Ista Hotel,1/1, Swami Vivekananda Rd., Ulsoor

The 'Indian Classics' food promotion is scheduled at Zaman restaurant, Ista Hotel. This offers aromatic Indian spices, with traditional cooking techniques. It also prepares fresh and delicious foods of North India.Timings:-7:00 PM - 11:00 PM.

Food Festival 'Weekend Sizzlers' at Zaman Restaurant

Ista Hotel,1/1, Swami Vivekananda Rd., Ulsoor

The food festival 'Weekend Sizzlers' on Saturdays is prepared at Zaman restaurant. This offers a number of food menus which includes barbequed chicken, grilled tournedos, tender lamb, tahina flavored cubes of cottage cheese and more. Enjoy with ta...

'Scintillating Sundays' Food Promotion at Zaman Restaurant

Ista Hotel, 1/1, Swami Vivekananda Rd., Ulsoor

The 'Scintillating Sundays' food promotion is programmed at Zaman restaurant, Ista Hotel. This provides food cuisines of delicious desserts, happy soups, baked breads, exotic salads grills, western Indian on Sundays. There is also oriental meal co...

Sunday Food Promotion at Civet @ ITPL Restaurant

Civet @ ITPL, Tech Park Mall

Civet @ ITPL Restaurant presents Sunday Food Promotion at Bangalore. It serves delicious dishes. If you want enjoy their delicious dishes, please join us.Timing: 12.00pm to 2.30pm.

Nightlife Revival Party at Kosmo Restaurant

18, Ali Askar Road, Off Cunningham Road Vasanth Nagar

Every Friday nightlife revival party will be organised by Kosmo Restaurant at Bangalore. They will revived with Havana Club bringing you the best in all kinds of music. Timing: 8.00pm to 11.00pm.

Electro DJ Night Party at Kosmo Restaurant Bangalore

18, Ali Askar Road, Off Cunningham Road Vasanth Nagar

Kosmo Restaurant presents Electro DJ Night Party on Every Monday in Bangalore. The DJ Kosmo will spin his magical web around you with his set of electro. If you want enjoy the dj night party, call us.Timing: 8.00pm to 11.00pm.

Question Mark - Quiz Show with Mark Rego at The Beach Restaurant

1211, 100 Feet Road, HAL 2nd Stage Indira Nagar

Come and rack your brains the quiz night with Mark Rego in Bangalore. Question Mark - Quiz Show will be held on Every Tuesdays The Beach Restaurant.Timing: 8.00pm to 11.30pm.Entry Charges for Rs. 500/- for couples & stags.

Ganeshotsav Festival

They say that a city's pulse is set by its rich art and culture. And for Pune, which has a history of art, architecture, music and the written word, the spirit of the city seems to never get lost. Each time of the year is associated with a festival and a reason for celebration. The Pune festival, known for its vibrantly rich appeal, sets off a series of celebrations every year.

The festival, which is part of the Ganeshotsav Festival, completes 22 years this year . Inaugurated on Saturday at

Lokmanya Tilak Auditorium, Kesariwada by K G Dharmadhikari, President, Gaanvardhan the stage seemed set for the curtain raiser of this year's chapter of the Pune Festival. With an aim to provide a platform to upcoming artists in the city, the festival started with Ugavate Taare, a talent show for child artistes in the age group of below 15, in which close to 300 children will be participating. The first two parts of Ugavate Taare was held from 9 am to 12 pm and from 5 pm to 8 pm on Saturday and the next part will be from 9 am to 12 pm today. Indradhanu, a show for artists from the age group of 15-25 years will be held in two sessions from 5 pm to 8 pm today and tomorrow.

Talking about the festival's long history, Krishnakant Kundale, chief coordinator of the Pune festival says, "I have been working for this programme since its inception. One of our aims is to attract tourists from abroad and other states to come and witness Maharashtra's culture. Apart from the usual performances, we have a range of programmes, right from car rallies to food festivals, that will begin once the festival picks up momentum, around mid-September."

The talent show for children, that began on Saturday, is in fact a wonderful way to encourage budding artistes. Rajkumar Raut, whose son 10 year old Piyush presented a povada, (a song of dedication) on Chhatrapati Shivaji Maharaj for the event says, "My son had performed the same povada in Mauritius for a Marathi conference. But performing here is altogether different. People appreciate you more because they connect, and this medium has encouraged my son a lot."

This talent search has really become popular in and around the city. Pratiksha Kate, whose daughter Payal has been participating in Ugavate Taare for three years now, shares, "My daughter is really happy to return to this stage every year. It helps her become more confident and inspired. And the kind of children who come truly showcases the potential and talent that the city has."

Sharing his thoughts about the festival, Ravindra Durve, Coordinator, Pune Festival says, "The first programme, which we have specifically for children, is actually very popular. We start getting entries for this as far back as June. Through this, upcoming artists in the age groups of 7-15 & 15-25 are given a platform and these people go on to achieve national & international fame."

Relish delicious brunch on weekends. At ofen, Road No 10, Banjara Hills On till September 10. Enjoy gilled and barbecqued food at Encounters, Taj Krishna. From September 10 onwards.

Choose Your Ingaredients Food

Choose your ingaredients and relish exotic Maongolian dishes. At Encounters, Taj Krishna, Banjara Hills. On till September 30, 7pm onwards.

Continental Food Fest At Often

Relish delicious continental dishes for brunch on weekends. At Often, Road No. 10, Banjara Hills. On till September 10.

Ramzan Food Feast At Hotel Golkonda

Feast on Ramzan buffet with specialties like haleem paya shorba sheer khurma and um ali. At Hotel Golkonda, Masab Tank, On till September 10.

Mongolian Food Festival At Taj Krishna

Choose your ingredients and relish exotic Mongolian dishes. At Encounters, Taj Krishna, Banjara Hills. On till September 30, 7 pm onwards.

Relish Appetizers At Syn Taj Deccan

Relish sushi's some wok finished appetizers, some green and red Thai curries for lunch. At Syn, Taj Deccan. From September 1 to 30.

Food Festival at Spar Outlets

Gourmets relish canned foods, Italian pasta, soups and sauces, wines from across 37 countries at a food festival. At Spar Outlets. On till September 12.

Food Festival At Haldi Novotel

Indulge in an array of beverages, soups, platter of different starters, main course and desserts. At Haldi, Novotel Shamshabad Airport. On till September 30, 6:30 pm to 11:30 pm.

Mongolian Food Festival

Choose your ingredients and relish exotic Mongolian dishes. At Encounters, Taj Krishna, Banjara Hills. On till September 30, 7 pm onwards.

Relish Sushi At Taj Deccan

Relish Sushi's, some work finished appetizers, some green and red Thai curries for lunch. At Syn, Taj Deccan. From September 1 to 30.

Food Festival At Haldi Novotel Hotel

Choose from an array of beverages, soups, platter of different starters, selection of main course and desserts. At Haldi, Novotel Hyderabad Airport, Shamshabad. From September 1 to 30 6:30 pm to 11:30 pm.

Various Food Festival At Spar Outlets

Relish Italian Pasta, canned foods, cookies, confectioneries, breakfast cereals and jams from 4 continents. At Spar Outlets. On till September 12.

Food Fest At Haldi Novotel Hotel

Make your own menu for a delightful feast with scrumptious dishes from across India. At Haldi, Novotel Hyderabad Airport. On till August 30, 6:30 pm.

Relish Sushi At Syn Taj Banjara

Relish Sushi's, some work finished appetizers, some green and red Thai curries for lunch. At Syn, Taj Deccan. From September 1 to 30.

Sushi And Red Thai Curries At Syn

Relish sushi's some work finished appetizers, some green and red Thai curries for lunch. At Syn, Taj Deccan. From September 1 to 30.

Relish Delicious Dishes At Kerala Food Festival

Gourmets relish delicious dishes of Gods own Country at Kerala Food Festival. On till August 29, from 7:30 pm.

Kerala Food Festival

Taj Krishna is hosting Kerala Food Festival offering delicacies of the region. At Encounters, from August 27 to September 5, for both lunch and dinner.

Sunda Brunch At Teppayanki

Head to Sunday brunch to relish sushi and dim sums and also check out cold meat, pizza and teppanyaki stations besides American barbeque and seafood. At Hotel Ista, Gachibowli

Food Festival Head to Sushi

Food Festival Head to Sushi and sparkling wine events to relish japanese cuisine besides tasting exotic wine. At Hotel Ista Gachibowli On till August 29.

Feast on Ramzan Buffet

Feast on Ramzan buffet WITH SPECIALITIES like haleem paya shorba sheer khurma and um ali. At Hotel Golkonda, Masab Tank, On till September 10.

Kerala Food Festival At Aditya Park Hotel

Gourmets relish delicious dishes of Gods own country at Kerala Food Festival. At Aditya Park, Ameerpet. On till August 29, from 7:30 pm.

Relish Italian Pasta at Spar Outlets

Relish Italian Pasta, canned food, cookies, confectionaries, breakfast cereals and jams from 4 continents. At Spar Outlets. On till September 12.

Relish Indian And Continental Cuisines

A chance to put together your own meal by choosing from 60 authentic and diverse Indian cuisines. At Haldi, Hotel Novotel, Shamshabad. On till August 31, 12 pm.

Sushi and Sparkling Wine

Head to 'Sushi and Sparkling Wine' event to relish Japanese Cuisine besides tasting exotic wine. At Hotel Ista, Gachibowli. On till August 29.

Relish Italian Pasta at Spar Outlets

Relish Italian Pasta, canned food, cookies, confectionaries, breakfast cereals and jams from 4 continents. At Spar Outlets. On till September 12.

Authetic Continental Cuisines at Often

Relish authentic Continental dishes for brunch in appropriate ambiance. At Often, Road No. 10, Banjara Hills.On till August 31, only on weekends.

Dim Sum Food Festival At Strings

Taj Banjara is hosting Dim Sum festival offering exotic Chinese cuisine. At Strings. On till August 29, 7:30 pm to 11:45 pm.

Food Fest at Hotel Novotel

Make your own menu for a delightful feast with scrumptious dishes from across India. At Haldi, Novotel Hyderabad Airport. On till August 30, 6:30 pm.

Kerala Food Festival

Gourmets relish delicious dishes of Gods own country at Kerala Food Festival. At Aditya Park, Ameerpet. On till August 29, from 7:30 pm.

Dim Sum Food Festival At Strings

Taj Banjara is hosting Dim Sum festival offering exotic Chinese cuisine. At Strings. On till August 29, 7:30 pm to 11:45 pm.

Kerala Food Festival At Hotel Aditya Park

On the eve of Onam festival, Hotel Aditya Park, Ameerpet, is hosting Kerala Food Festival offering delicacies of the region. On till August 29, from 7:30 pm.

Celebrate This Onam With Onam Sadya

Celebrate this Onam with Onam Sadya offering dishes like parupu, pulchery, avuvar, apalam and thoranam. At Utupura Kerala Restaurant, Road No.10, Banjara Hills. On till August 23, 11 am onwards.

Indulge in Dishes at Bidri

Indulge in dishes like dal bati, churma, mirchi bada, desi murg and degchi sula at Bidri, Hotel Marriott. On till August 31, 7:30 pm.

Choose From 60 Indian Cuisines

A chance to put together your own meal by choosing from 60 authentic and diverse Indian cuisines. At Haldi, Hotel Novotel, Shamshabad. On till August 31, 12 pm.

Relish Continental Cuisine at Often

Relish exotic continental cuisine in appropriate ambiance for brunch. At Often, Road No. 10, Banjara Hills. From August 20, only on weekends.

Celebrate this Onam with Onam Sadya

Celebrate this Onam with Onam Sadya offering dishes like parupu, pulcherry, avuar, apalam and thoranam. At Utupura Kerala Restaurant, Road No. 10, Banjara Hills. On August 23, 11 am onwards.

SHANDONG FOOD FESTIVAL AT TAJ KRISHNA

Taj Krishna is hosting shandong food festival offering exotic Chinese cuisinc at Golden Dragon. On till today, 12:30 pm onwards.

'Sushi and Sparkling Wine' - At Hotel Ista

Head to 'Sushi and sparkling Wine' Event to relish Japanese cuisine and taste exotic wine. At Hotel Ista, Gachibowli. On till August 29, 12 pm to 3:30 pm.

Make Your Own Menu at Haldi, Novotel

Make your own menu for a delightful feast with scrumptious dishes from across India. At Haldi, Novotel Hyderabad Airport. On till August 30, 6:30 pm.

Relish Various Dishes at Bidri

Relish dal-bati churma, Jodhpuri mirchi bada, desi murg and degchi sula at Rajasthan Food Festival. At Bidri, Hotel Marriott. On till Augsut 31, 7:30 pm.

Food and Drinks a Head To Sushi

Food and Drinks a Head To Sushi and Sparkling wine event to relish Japanese cuising and taste exotic wine. At Hotel Ista Gachibowli, 12pm to 3.30pm.

Food and Drink Celebrare with Onam Sadya

Food and Drink Celebrare with Onam Sadya this onam offering dishes like parupa pulchery avuar apalam and thoranam. At utupura kerala Resturand Road No 10. Banjara hills. On August 23, 11am onwards.

60 Authetic and Indian Cuisines

A chance to put together your own meal by choosing from 60 authentic and diverse Indian cuisines. At Haldi, Hotel Novotel, Shamshabad. On till August 31, 12 pm.

Shandong Food Festival at Taj Krishna

Taj Krishna is hosting Shandong food festival offering exotic, Chinese cuisine. At Golden Dragon. On till August 20, 12:30 pm to 3 pm.

Bidri Restaurant is Hosting Rajasthan Food Festival

Taste dal-bati churma, Jodhpuri mirchi bada, desi mrug and degchi sula at Rajasthan Food Festival. At Bidri, Hotel Marriott. On till August 31, 7:30 pm.

Onam Dishes at Utupura Kerala Restaurant

Celebrate this Onam with Onam Sadya offering dishes like, Parupu, pulchery, avuar, apalam and thoranam. At Utupura Kerala Restaurant, Road No. 10, Banjara Hills. On August 23, 11 am onwards.

Lip Smacking Delicacies at Quality Inn Pearl Hotel

Gourmets indulge in lip smacking delicacies in Italian, Mexican and pan Asian dishes for lunch buffet. At Quality Inn Pearl Hotel, Acharya Marg, Gachibwoli. On till August 14.

Rajasthani Food Festival at Hotel Marriott

Taste dal-bati churma, Jodhpuri mirchi bada, desi murg and degchi sula at Rajasthan Food Festival. At Bidri, Hotel Marriott. On till August 31, 7:30 pm.

Onam Dishes Food Festival At Utupura

Celebrate this Onam with Onam Sadya offering dishes like parupu, pulcherry, avuar apalam and thoranam. At utupura Kerala Restaurant, Road No. 10, Banjara Hills. On August 23, 11 am onwards.

A Delightful Feast at Airport

Make your own menu for a delightful feast with scrumptious dishes from across India. Airport. On till August 30, 6:30 pm.

Regional Food Fest at Deori

Relish regional delicacies like idiyappam, paniyaram, vellai paniyaram, karuppatti paniyaram. At Deori, Hotel Ista, Gachibowli. On till August 15 at 7 pm.

Italian and Mexican Food Festival

Indulge in Italian, Mexican and pan Asian dishes for lunch buffet. At Quality Inn Pearl, Acharya Marg Gachibowli. On till August 15.

Rajasthan Food Festival at Taj Deccan

Savour dal-bati churma, Jodhpuri mirchi bada, desi murg and degchi sula at Rajasthan Food Festival. At Bidri, Hotel Marriott. From August 12 to 31, 7:30 pm.

Food Festival at Calcutta Cabin

Relish dishes like ilish jhal, begun diye. Food Festival. At Calcutta Cabin, Road No.1, Jubilee Hills. On till August 15.

Chettinad Food Festival

Hotel Ista, Gachibowli, is hosting 'Chettinad Food Festival' offering specialties of the region in ala carte menu. At Deori on till August 15, 7 pm onwards.

Hilsa Food Festival

Relish dishes like ilish jhal, begun diye and bhapa ilish at 'Hilsa Food Festival'. At Calcutta Cabin, Road No.1. Jubilee Hills. On till August 15.

Mughalai Food Festival

City gourmets indulge in lip smacking delicacies in Mughalai Food Festival. At Haldi, Novotel Hyderabad Airport, Shamshabad. On till August 15, at 6:30 pm.

Rajasthani Food Festival at Bidri

Taste dal-bati churma, Jodhpuri mirchi bada, desi murg and dagchi sula at Rajasthan Food Festival. At Bidri Hotel Marriott. From August 12 to 31, 7:30 pm.

Chettinad Food Festival at Ista

Hotel Ista, Gachibowli is hosting 'Chettinad Food Festival' that offers specialitics of the region in a la carte menu. At Deori. From August 4 to 15, 7 pm onwards.

Rajasthani Food Festival

Taste dal-bati churna, Jodhpuri mirchi bada, desi murg and degchi sula in Rajasthan Food Festival. At Bidri, Hotel Marriott. From August 12 to 31, 7:30 pm.

Food Fest at Mughalai Hyderabad

Gourmets indulge in lip smacking delicacies in Mughalai Hyderabad Airport, Shamshabad. On till August 15, at 6:30 pm.

Rajasthani Food Festival at Bidri

Taste dal-bati churna, Jodhpuri mirchi bada, desi murg and degchi sula in Rajasthan Food Festival. At Bidri, Hotel Marriott. From August 12 to 31, 7:30 pm.

Sea Food Festival at Alcazar Plaza

Relish dinner buffet with chicken curry, sea food specialties and much more. At The Grand Wok, Alcazar Plaza, Road No. 1, Banjara Hills. On till August 7, between 7 pm to 11 pm.

Food Feast at Hotel Novotel

Make your own menu for a delightful feast with scrumptious dishes from across India. At Haldi, Novotel Hyderabad Airport. On till August 30, 6:30 pm.

Dinner Buffet at Alcazar Plaza

Relish dinner buffet with chicken curry, sea food specialties and much more. At The Grand Wok, Alcazar Plaza, Road No. 1, Banjara Hills. On till August 7, between 7 pm to 11 pm.

'Chettinad Food Festival' at Ista

Hotel Ista, Gachibowli is hosting 'Chettinad Food Festival' that offers specialities of the region in a la carte menu. At Deori. From August 4 to 15, 7 pm onwards.

Delightful Feast at Novotel's Haldi

Make your own menu for a delightful feast with scrumptious dishes from across India. At Haldi, Novotel Hyderabad Airport. On till August 30, 6:30 pm.

Kerala Food Festitival at Salzburg

Head 'Kerala Food Festival' to relish exotic dishes like appam, Kerala Meen curry, kovakaya thoranam and much more. At Salzburg Street, Best Western Castle. On till August 1.

Express Lunch at Hotel Ista

Relish express lunch with exotic dishes. At Collage, Hotel Ista, Gachibowli. From August 1-30.

Lunch Buffet at One Place Hotel

Relish lunch buffet with chicken biryani, tandoori rotis and paneer butter masala. At One Place Hotel, KPHB Colony. On till July 30, 12 pm onwards.

Enjoy Sushi at Taj Deccan

Enjoy Sushi, some exotic appetizers besides green and red Thai curries and lots more for lunch. AT Syn Asian Grill & Bar, Taj Deccan. On till July 30.

Bruchetta Festival at Taj Banjara

City Gourmets head to Bruchetta Festival to taste some delicacies. At Hotel Taj Banjara, Banjara Hills. On till July. On till July 30.

Mughalai Food Festival

Satiate your palate with exotic dishes in Mughalai Food Festival. AT Haldio,Hotel Novotel Airport, Shamshabad. From August 1to 15.

Rice Food Festival at Westin

Experience a variety of biryanis, rice items, chicken and mutton dishes. At Westin Hyderabad, Madhapur. On till July 31, at 12.30 pm.

Relish Lunch Buffet at One Place Hotel

Relish lunch buffet with chicken biryani, tandoori rotis and paneer butter masala. At One Place Hotel, KPHB Colony. On till July 30, 12 pm onwards.

'Kerala Food Festival' at Salzburg

Head 'Kerala Food Festival' to relish exotic dishes like appam, Kerala Meen curry, kovakaya thoranam and much more. At Salzburg Street, Best Western Castle. On till August 1.

Chicken and Mutton Food Fest at Katriya

Relish a dinner buffet with chicken and mutton curries, tikka and fries. At Orchid, Hotel Katriya, Raj Bhavan Road. On till July 31, 7:30 pm onwards.

Kerala Food Festival At Salzburg

Best western Amrutha Castle is hosting Kerala Food Festival offering dishes like morapanjyam, appam Malabar mutton and Kerala Fish curries. AT Salzburg Street. On till August 1.

Biryani Food Fest at Westin

Experience a variety of biryanis, rice items, chicken and mutton dishes. At Westin Hyderabad, Madhapur. On till July 31, at 12.30 pm.

Express Lunch at Hotel Ista

Savour express lunch with Indian & Continental dishes. At Hotel Ista, Gachibowli. On till July 31.

Dinner Buffet at Hotel Orchid

Relish dinner buffet with chicken and mutton curries tikka and fries. At Orchid, Hotel Katirya, Raj Bhavan Road On till July 31, 7.30 pm onwards.

Relish Multicuisine at MoMo Cafe

City Gourmets savour and Relish Thai, Chinese and Malaysian dishes at Asian Street food Fiesta. At MoMo Cafe, Hotel Marriott. From July 7 to 25.

Breakfast Buffet at Green Park Hotel

Enjoy an elaborate breakfast buffet offering a variety of puris, vadas and much more. At Green Park Hotel Begumpet. On July 24 and 25.

Relish Express Lunch

Relish express lunch with Indian & Continental dishes.At Hotel Ista, Gachibowli. On till July 31.

Midnight Buffet at Hotel Kakatiya

City Gourmets savor biryani and kebabs besides Indian, Continental and Chinese cuisines for midnight buffet. At Hotel Kakatiya Sherton, Begumpet. On till July 30 and 31.

Reslish Chinese Cuisine

Relish Chinese cuisine including chicken peel, phuket fish for lunch. At Wang's Kitchen Restaurant. Madhapur. On til July 31.

Enjoy Dinner Buffet at Katriya

Enjoy diner buffet with chicken and mutton curries, tikka besides soups and desserts. At Orchid, Katriya Hotel Raj Bhavan Road, On till July 31, from 7:30 pm.

Thalis along with Desserts at Westin

Experience a variety of 'Thalis' along with desserts, sweets and much more. At Westin Hyderabad, Madhapur. On till July 31, at 12 pm.

Express Lunch at Hotel Ista

Relish express lunch with Indian & Continental dishes. At Hotel Ista, Gachibowli. On till July 31.

Enjoy Sushi at Syn Asian Grill & Bar

Enjoy Sushi, some exotic appetizers besides green and red Thai curries and lots more for lunch. At Syn Asian Grill & Bar, Taj Deccan. On till July 21.

Enjoy Sushi at Syn Asian Grill & Bar

Enjoy Sushi, some exotic appetizers besides green and red Thai curries and lots more for lunch. At Syn Asian Grill & Bar, Taj Deccan. On till July 21.

Thai Chinese and Malaysian Food Fest

City Gourmets savour and Relish Thai, Chinese and Malaysian dishes at Asian Street food Fiesta. At MoMo Cafe, Hotel Marriott. From July 7 to 25.

Sizzler Food Festival

Head to sizzler Food Festival, a-la-carte, to relish vegetarian and non-vegetarian sizzlers.At Hotel Green park, from July 14 to 24, 7:30 pm onwards.

South Ibndian Dosa Festiva

Best Western Amrutha Castle is hosting a Dosa Festival offering masala, rava and varied other dosas. At The Salzburg Street. From July 1-20.

Food Festival at Westin Hyderabad

Experience a variety of thalis along with desserts, sweets and much more. At Westin Hyderabad, Madhapur. On till July 31, at 12 pm.

Indian And Continental Lunch

Relish an exquisite Indian and Continental lunch at Hotel Ista, Gachibowli. On till July 31.

Thalis and Desserts at Westin

Experience a variety of thalis along with desserts, sweets and much more. At Westin Hyderabad, Madhapur. On till July 31, at 12 pm.

Food Fest at Waterside Cafe

Enjoy exotic cuisine at Waterside Café till 4:00 pm on 25th July at Taj Banjara.

Indian and Continental Lunch at Ista

Relish an exquisite Indian and Continental lunch at Hotel Ista, Gachibowli. On till July 31.

Ice Cream feast at Taj Deccan

Celebrate World Ice Cream day by indulging your love for Ice Creams at Taj Deccan fom 15th-18th July, 5 pm to 7 pm onwards.

Chapter 4

Yummy and Delicious Food

Had my first grape harvest this year. What a rush - the vines grew wildly and rampantly and disgorged the most marvelously tasting merlots and concords.

I had ignored the vines, letting them overgrow in winter and never watering.

in the Spring and Summer. Tall grass covered them, wisteria overshadowed them and a blue rose or two stabbed them.

Amongst all the competition, they rose to occasion, climbing their fellows reaching for the sun. The calm before the storm... riotous grapes burst from tiny clusters of bubbles.

One of the most interesting things about these grapes - they healed. They took away my appetite for anything unhealthy, and the next morning I awoke refreshed and glowy.

Never used any pesticides, never did anything to the soil. In fact, thought the soil was beyond redemption. Who knows the lead content from the past But, one thing is for sure - there's been no chemicals for over 12 years, winter rains have washed the soil repeatedly, and not a bit of fertilizer has ever been applied.

Don't know which was more fun - eating these globules of goodness or taking their picture.

Grow your own...

Notes: Bought the original vines from local hardware store. Lucked out - they were a spectacular variety. You can order online. I would buy heirloom these days... then test.

I would plant grapes around any house I would have - vines and vines. Would trellis them, arbors galore. Life couldn't be sweeter.

This delicious natural old world recipe will surprise you - the batter will be particularly light and crispy. The fish skin will add flavor. The fresher the fish, the sweeter, more tender and flaky the fish.

Fish and chips may be one of the dishes that never gets old. Today, high quality fish is becoming increasingly rare due to over fishing. Unfortunately, many fish varieties are no longer available. Enjoy in moderation, and encourage sustainable Net fishing.

INGREDIENTS

1 3/4 Cups of Unbleached Flour

1 Teaspoon Natural Baking Soda

2 Small Pinches Sea Salt

2 Pounds Fresh Whitefish with Skin - Cod, Halibut, Haddock, Flounder, Perch cut into serving sized pieces.

1 Cup Ice Water OR

1/2 Cup Ice Water and

1/2 Cup Cold Effervescent English Beer

(If you prefer to eliminate beer, increase water to 1 Cup)

Peanut or High Quality Oil or Natural Organic Lard, minimum 1 inch deep in pan, 3 inches in pot for deep

FRYING

2 Pounds Peeled and Dried Potatoes cut into small strips

Barley Malt Vinegar

Instructions

Mix flour, Salt and Water into a smooth batter. This can be accomplished by making a well in the center of the flour and gradually and gently stir in the ice water. When smooth, add baking soda and gently stir. "Rest" the batter in the refrigerator for at least 45 minutes to an hour.

Make sure fillets are dry. Dredge in a little flour and salt.

Heat the oil till drop of water sizzles and pops. Dip the fish into the batter and fry until golden brown, aproximately 5 minutes. Drain on wire rack, keep warm in oven.

The Potato

Deep fry potatoes in oil into golden brown, serve with fish and season to taste with vinegar and salt.

Notes About Making the Best English Chips

Ah yes... the secret to making the perfect English Chips. First of all, unlike American Potato Chips, English chips are not wafer thin circles, crunchy all the way through. The English Chip is basically a fat American french fry. Or, vice versa...

First of all, consider the potato itself. Each variety has good and not as good points. Some are fluffy, others silky. Some mash nicely, others are best boiled.

For chips, the best varieties of potatoes will fry up tender, rich and fluffy on the inside and crisply golden brown on the outside. They will soak oil creamily, and taste like heaven. Some even like them soft, a bit chewy, soggy, but crisped on the outside. Interesting!

If the fat is superb, then perhaps any amount will seem acceptable. Nothing is worse than old, rancid oil or fat. Plus, it's terrible for you.

In America, organic russets do the trick quite nicely and are common.

The secret potato tricks are these:

Soaking in icy water with a dash of salt in the fridge for several hours, then draining and drying.

Frying twice

Using the finest natural organic lard

If no lard, then organic filtered peanut oil

Fry up once at lower heat. Then, when ready to serve, fry at high heat to golden, perfect brown. Sprinkle with the best natural salt and fine malt vinegar.

No wonder fish and chips is a national favorite. Add salad, perhaps a bit of fruit ice for dessert. Incredible.

THE SALAD

The secret to a delicious fresh green salad is hidden in the name - fresh. The more recently the greens were picked, the more pure and delicate the flavors and the tender with full crispness and satisfying crunch.

Another major secret is the dressing. Any delicious dressing can make a mediocre salad taste good.

But, when you marry fresh greens and a great dressing, nirvana is attained.

Ingredients

1/4 Head Green Leaf Lettuce

1/4 Head Iceberg Lettuce

4 Large Romaine Lettuce Leaves

2 Small or 1 Large Tomato

3 oz. Your Favorite Cheese

Chopped Scallions (Optional)

Finely Sliced Rings of Red Onion

Your Favorite Fresh Baked Croutons

Organic Apple Cider or Malt Vinegar

2 Tbsp. Light Organic Olive Oil or High Quality Vegetable Oil

1 Teaspoon Organic Raw Sugar to Taste

Sea or Natural Non-Heat Treated Salt

1/4 Finely Minced Garlic Clove (Optional)

Fresh Ground Pepper

Fresh Finely Chopped Herbs - Use Sparingly

Particular Favorites

Oregano, Thyme, Basil, Tarragon, Rosemary, Sage

Note: Freshly snipped home grown herbs taste remarkably different than dried seasoning herbs.

Instructions

Tear Greens into bite sized pieces. You can chop them without a problem as well; they will still taste just as good. Once it was considered bad form to chop salad greens. This may be possibly due to the use of non-stainless steel utensils.

Mix salt, finely chopped herbs, fresh ground pepper, sugar, garlic and vinegar and mix gently. Set Aside. Toss greens with Olive Oil. Add a tablespoon water to the herb mixture, stir and toss into the greens. Top with Scallions, Croutons, Red Onion Rings. Serve immediately with your hot fish and potatoes.

A Little Note About Wheat

Wheat is a very nutritious and long-storing grain. In my humble opinion, wheat allergies may very well be due to the processing and chemical adulteration of wheat in recent decades. Not due to the wheat itself.

ESPECIALLY if true organic natural NON-genetically modified kernels are used. Now this is just my personal thought. :

Money Saving

Did you know that you can simmer your grains and feed a family of four with pennies rather than dollars

These days, bread is somewhat a luxury with a medium loaf ranging from $2.50 to $5.00 each. When you consider the nutrient value, bread is mostly water, crushed processed flour and additives.

We all love bread. But these days, we're very much into preserving our pennies and watching our budget. With the wintry cold, (a brisk 55 degrees in Southern California :), there's nothing better than a hot bowl of whole grain delicately seasoned with a delightful meat broth.

VEGETARIAN STYLE

Personally, I love my simmered whole grains seasoned with a lovely selection of vegetables and perhaps some herbs and dash of organic butter, the butter being my concession to the world of meaty eating.

Today, we're all very full, we feel wonderful, and a warm bowl of tender chewy nuggets of wheat goodness absolutely hit the spot!

Happy Holidays with "Delicious Holiday Wheat Slow Cooked with Fresh Organic Chicken!"

RECIPE

So Simple and So Delicious - Nutty, Tender Yet Chewy - Full of Fiber and Wholesomeness - a filling, warm and satisfying wintry meal :

Ingredients

1 1/2 - 2 pounds of Organic Winter Wheat Berries

2 fresh whole organic chicken legs with bone in

Sprig of fresh thyme from your little kitchen window herb garden

Sprig of sage if you have it, otherwise a 1/3 teaspoon seasoning

Utah Mineral Salt to Taste AFTER preparation

Pinch fresh ground organic pepper if you must

Instructions

For greater deliciousness and nutrition, first soak whole grain organic wheat for at least 24 hours. This will lower cooking times and release the magic of enzymes and the beginnings of the sprout of life, greatly enhancing the availability of nutrients within the grain.

Bring 3/4 water filled crockpot to steamy heat on high. Add the wheat, making sure it's quite submerged beneath the surface of the water. Then, fill the pot with water almost to the top.

Too much water Spoon out! :

Let cook overnight on LOW, depending upon your crockpot. We use a $17 Procter Silex pot that we got from Target. (We had given away our original nice pot, thinking we'd eat everything raw. Not happening!:)

In the morning, you will be greeted with a delicious fragrance and perhaps the most substantial hot breakfast you could imagine.

So good, you'll have more for dinner, and take some for lunch.

Did you know that something so simple could be so good

Try this, then please let me know if you agree or disagree!

Rutabaga has the creamy rich texture of both russet and golden potatoes together and the delicate flavor of cabbage and radish all at once. That is, if you buy the rutagbagas I did.

I always buy organic ($1.89 a pound) because they just taste so home garden fresh. I don't cook a huge amount, you know... less is best!

If young grumpy guys like rutabaga, if small kids like it, then most likely you and yours will, too. :)

If you don't, give me your helping. I will eat your rutabagas. I will eat them ALL up.

RECIPE

Ingredients (Serves 2)

1 Large Organic Rutabaga or Two Medium Rutabagaslarge organic rutabaga or two medium rutabagas

Fresh Organic Sweet Butter

Natural Salt

Fresh Ground Organic Pepper

INSTRUCTIONS

Thoroughly wash and scrub your rutabaga. Cut off the stem, rootbits and tough areas.

Toss lightly with a 1/3 inch pat of fresh organic butter, a sprinkle of natural non-heat treated mineral salt or kosher salt and some fresh ground pepper to taste. Serve steaming hot.

That's it! Your rutabaga strips should be golden brown, buttery rich and silken. If fresh and organic, it will have a delicate flavor and a creamy potato-like texture.

Your rutabaga is wonderful for wintry holiday fare. Goes well with sweet potatoes, peas and onions and other traditional fare.

VARIATIONS:

Vegetable Oil instead of butter - Toss lightly with Planter's Peanut Oil or Organic Peanut Oil instead of butter if you prefer.

Serve with a dollop of sour cream and fresh chopped parsley.

Incredibly delicious, filling, rich and nutritious - Feeds 20 for about $5.00

Wash and gently boil the following, separately: Rice with dash of butter and natural salt till fluffy separate Vermicelli until soft, drain and toss with oil and salt Fava beans until tender, then mash till lumpy (Canned, drained, simmered for 10 minutes is fine) Black Lentils until tender

Garbanzo beans (canned, drained and simmered for 10 minutes is fine).

Simmer a sauce of tomato paste, dash chili powder, vinegar (adds sour, your choice), cumin, cardamon, tiny dash cinnamon, black pepper, salt, Olive Oil. Season to taste. Add several cloves of garlic if you wish. Garlic is more Moraccan than Egyptian, they say.

Thinly slice and finely chop onions, fry in plenty of your favorite oil (mine is Organic filtered Peanut Oil) until brown and crisp - they will make your cooking area smell divine.

Slice a boiled egg into thin slivers and cut crossways.

Fresh slices lemon or lime.

Red pepper spice, Black Pepper.

Layer your small tub, bowl or dish as follows:

2 heaping tbsps Rice

2 heaping tbsps Vermicelli

1 heaping tbsp Lentils

1 tbsp Dash Red Sauce

2 tbsps Dashes Lumpy fava bean gravy

1 heaping tbsp sprinkling of tender chickpeas (garbanzos)

1 tbsp Dash Red Sauce Dash Red Sauce

Giant heaping tbsp (Plenty!) of Onion Bits with Delicious Oil

(Use organic oil so you don't feel guilty)

(Don't worry - oil is only 100 calories a tablespoon,

so a teaspoon is only 33 calories)

Top with heaping tsp of chopped egg

Perhaps squeeze of lime or lemon, dash black pepper

Serve with small chunk of flat brown bread

This dish will lodge in your stomach like a mortar and last you the entire day. You should feel sustained and strong.

If you ate this everyday, you would live long enough to build... a pyramid! These dishes are beloved in Egypt, where they originated from India and were adapted to Egyptian tastes and palates. The Brits call the Indian dish, Kitcheree.

NOTE Separate out the fava bean stew and serve with bread, sauce, fried onions, boiled eggs and plenty of warm flat brown bread. Yummm Oh, as Rachel Ray would say! :)

Meanwhile, while I drool, it's late. Off to bed... dreaming of Anthony Bourdain and his immemorable trip to Egypt.

And the Promise of Dinner... Dusk is a special time of day. Years ago, someone gave me a word in German to describe that certain time of day when twilight falls and the day's mood darkens and ushers in a new sense of excitement. Perhaps, the special orange, gold, salmon and silvery light that heralds... the promise of family and supper

Whatever it is, I love dusk at first sight of distant stars in the deep blue depths of space. There's a new excitement - warm orange lights aglow, sparkling glitter on distant horizons, promises of warm conviviality to come.

You can imagine families settling down for dinner, sharing moments of their day, napkins tucked, mother rustling in the warm kitchen, father loosening his tie while little ones chatter excitedly in his ear. Well! We're off to supper ourselves... but first, a quick announcement that we've done a Weight Loss Page about a special diet noodle. We decided to create this special page as we are certain that these amazing noodles, centuries old, can help many people with weight loss.

Being a cosmopolitan city Delhi food having various foods tastes as well. Since food is something that most people do take seriously and also that, a good experience in a restaurant becomes a lingering memory and a bad one sticks out like a sore thumb. New Delhi restaurants serve a wide variety of cuisines ranging from Italian,

French, and Korean food to German food, you can easily find out the favorites of many states like Bengali food, Andhara food, and Gujrati food.

Another Low Calorie Granola

And their granola is oh-so yummy and contains seventy percent less fat than other traditional granola. Now if you know me at all and have been following my blog, then you know that any product that passes my taste test AND has so much less fat than other options is going to be high on my list of products that I recommend. Yes, Galaxy Granola gets high accolades from me. Hooray for a new low calorie snack and low calorie breakfast option!

And what Galaxy Granola doesn't have is equally as impressive. In addition to having no oil, this yummy granola has no artificial ingredients, no corn syrup, and no processed sugar - and no saturated fats or trans-fats. A quarter cup serving of my favorite Galaxy Granola (vanilla almond, and yes, it contains whole glazed almonds with the granola bits) is only 120 calories, 2 grams of fat, no sodium, and 4 grams of protein (so only 2 weight watchers points!). You can also choose from flavors like "not sweet" vanilla (don't worry, it's still naturally sweet), cranberry orange and raspberry (contains delicious freeze-dried raspberries) at 115 calories per serving.

I like to eat this granola on its own as a crunchy and healthy low calorie snack alone or with chocolate cocoa nibs, but I also like to sprinkle it over Fage yogurt with a handful of fruit, like blueberries, frozen bananas, or sliced strawberries. Or, even as a topping on low calorie ice cream! Or, by itself with low calorie almond milk for breakfast. This is a chewy and flavorful granola that you will adore.

And if you don't want to take my word for it, Galaxy Granola is also giving away free samples of two flavors of their granola by simply filling out the form found on their site. You can also find Galaxy Granola at your local Whole Foods market where I buy mine, or online from Amazon.

Benefits of Protein and High Protein Diets

Although I'm not a huge fan of diet plans like Atkins or South Beach, a high protein diet does offer lots of benefits that cannot be overlooked - and lots of people have success with this type of eating plan. A diet that is high in protein ensures that your body gets the protein it needs, obviously. Protein is necessary for building muscles, which is, as you know, what you are aiming for when you lose fat. And when you build muscle, keep in mind that the body has to work harder to not only build muscle, but muscle also uses up more energy (calories).

Other tissues, like your hair, skin, bones, blood, and cartilage - basically all of the cells in your body, need protein. A diet that is high in protein and low in carbohydrates will force your body to burn fat (thus the theory behind Atkins), which puts the body into what is known as ketosis. Fat is melted away and broken down for energy. This is the biggest and most obvious benefit of a high protein diet plan.

But in lieu of eating cheese and meat, there are some great protein options that are not all that unhealthy. Soy milk (one cup equals seven grams of protein), oatmeal, brown rice, eggs, tofu, lentils, and muesli all are abundant sources of protein, and foods like broccoli and potatoes have some protein in them too. You can also add protein to your diet with low calorie protein powder that can be mixed into a healthy low calorie smoothie. There are also some great (and organic) peanut butters on the market. You may recall that I reviewed a delicious low calorie peanut butter (PB2) that can be tossed into the blender with your favorite smoothie or stirred into some plain, non-fat yogurt, which, by the way, can contain as much as twelve grams of protein per serving, depending on the brand you buy. And for snacking, crunchy foods like flax seeds, soy nuts, almonds, healthy nut mixes, and pumpkin seeds provide about eight grams of protein per quarter cup. Or, if you don't like nuts, you can snack on string cheese, or edamame.

Yummy Ideas with Vegetable Broth

One way that I like to reduce the calories in dishes that I make (while still keeping them yummy) is by adding vegetable broth. I particularly like Swanson's Certified Organic Vegetable Broth, it is made with certified organic vegetables and is completely free from fat and MSG while having one-third less salt than Swanson's original vegetable broth. You can also make your own broth, which is more fun and a whole lot more economical - plus you definitely know what's going into it!

I like to add vegetable broth in dishes that include whole grain rice, or when sautéing vegetables in my wok. I have also been known to roast vegetables in the oven using vegetable broth. Just take a few medium red potatoes, some celery, baby carrots, a rutabaga and a couple of red onions and add a few cloves of thinly sliced garlic, and a tablespoon of rosemary - and place everything in a shallow baking pan. Toss a tablespoon of extra virgin olive oil in the mix. Then pour a cup (or more, depending on the number of vegetables) over the veggies, and roast at 425 for about 25 minutes, or until your veggies are tender when you stick a fork in them. Yummy!

To make your own yummy broth, place your favorite veggies in a stock pot and cover with water. The vegetables you choose should be chopped, but you don't need to peel them. Actually, the skins are chock full of flavor, too, as well as vitamins. You can use onions, celery, carrots, mushrooms (makes a dark broth especially with portabellos), and parsnips, spinach, bell peppers, tomatoes, turnips, zucchini, leeks, or even veggie scraps, like cauliflower or broccoli stems, potato peels, or the ends of green beans. You can add fresh herbs, garlic, or even wine to your broth. Add salt and pepper to taste (I prefer to make mine without salt, and just season it later when I use it). You can also use Mrs. Dash or other salt substitutes if you wish. Heat until boiling - and then lower the heat and allow simmering for about an hour. Remove from heat and allow time for cooling before pouring the liquid through a strainer.

If you make more broth than you can use, you can always freeze it for later. I sometimes freeze this broth in ice trays, which allows me to take out just a few cubes for a dish for two, or more as I need it. You can also cook your rice in broth instead of water, which gives the rice a delicious flavor or replace the milk in your mashed potatoes with broth instead.

Although I love the Swanson's broth, I also like that I can control everything that goes into the mix when I make my own. And I can replace the chicken or beef stock that is called for in many soup recipes with this all-veggie broth, which lowers the calories and makes it perfect for vegetarians.

Heart Thrive Bars - Low Calorie, Low Fat, Super Filling, & Healthy.

A Vegan Energy Bar that's also good for Your Heart! Finally, an energy bar that I can feel good recommending to my loyal readers! I am always on the lookout for food options that are not only good but that are good for you. And the Heart Thrive Bars fit the bill. This is a great energy bar that is perfect for anyone who is concerned about their health and looking to add whole grains to their diet for a yummy, low fat and high-fiber snack. These bars offer the ideal balance of protein, carbohydrates and fat - and they help prevent the quick rise in blood sugar that can end up making you feel hungry faster with other bars. (That makes them just what the doctor ordered for diabetics, too, by the way).

One reason that I'm particularly drawn to Heart Thrive Bars, other than the fact that they taste so good, is that their number one ingredient - oats - is the first food that the FDA has allowed to be attached to health claims. Yep, the FDA says that oats, as part of a diet low in saturated fat and cholesterol, may reduce the risk of heart disease. So, since Heart Thrive Bars are both free from cholesterol and abundant in oats - they make the best snack for those who are concerned with heart health.

Each Heart Thrive Bar provides you with thirty percent of your total RDA for fiber, protein and calcium (contains as much calcium as an eight-ounce glass of milk). They contain no trans-fats, no cholesterol, no wheat, and no GMO. For those on an all vegan diet, this is a wonderful and tasty way to get your protein in each day. And these bars are made from ingredients with a low glycemic index that allows them to metabolize slowly, which keeps you feeling full longer - and that helps you sustain your energy for a longer period of time.

There are currently seven flavors of Heart Thrive Bars, including raisin, chocolate chip, date, apple, poppy seed (my personal favorite!), cranberry, and apricot. And they are made with all-natural, vegan ingredients, including oats, soy, dried fruit, natural fruit juices, and sweetened with brown rice syrup. Each bar has less than 167 calories, and most are merely 2 weight watchers points. I buy mine at Whole Foods but I've seen them at other natural food stores as well.

Dreyers Cookies and Cream Low Calorie Ice Cream.

Now you may recall that I recommended a low calorie cookies-and-cream shake from Spiru-tein in previous post, and yes, this is one of my favorite flavors! (After all, when you blend the impeccable deliciousness of chocolate sandwich cookies with the goodness of ice cream, the result is a taste combination that is irresistible). I also recently reviewed Arctic Zero ice cream (only 150 calories per PINT), and in a previous post I recommended the low-calorie mint ice cream sandwiches from So-Delicious. But what's not to love about ice cream You don't have to be a kid standing on the street corner waiting for the ice cream truck to be a big fan of this chilly and yummy treat. Especially when you're eating Dryer's Light Cookies-and-Cream Ice Cream that has fifty percent less fat and thirty percent fewer calories than your traditional ice cream choices - but is still just as yummy.

Each ½ cup serving contains 130 calories and gives you a great deal of the traditional ice cream taste with just 4 grams of fat per serving (so 3 weight watchers points).

For an unbelievable low calorie milkshake, I've found that blending Almond Milk with ½ cup of Dryer's Cookies-and-Cream ice cream creates a milkshake so rich and delicious, you'll think it is much more fattening than it really is.

Here's my take on a low calorie Cookies-and-Cream Shake (4 delicious weight watchers points):

½ cup Dryer's Cookies-and-Cream Light Ice Cream

1 cup almond milk or coconut milk

1 cup crushed ice cubes

Put all in blender and puree until smooth. Sit outside and savor as this is the perfect summer time treat!

Tuesday, August 24, 2010

Low-Calorie Banana Waffles

If you're watching your waistline, chances are good that waffles are currently not a word that is found in your vocabulary. I have modified my grandma's traditional banana buckwheat waffles to be low-cal and high on taste. By simply replacing the milk in the original recipe with soy milk and the eggs in her recipe with low calorie egg replacement, I have created one breakfast that I especially enjoy. We have even had this for a low calorie dinner, too, or as a decadent morning brunch. The recipe below serves six and each serving has just 258 calories and 7 fat grams while providing 8 grams of protein and 4 grams of fiber (5 weight watchers points)!

INGREDIENTS:

1 1/2 tsp. baking powder

1 cup buckwheat flour

1 cup flour

1 Tbs. maple syrup (you'll need more for serving, if desired)

1/2 tsp. salt

1/4 tsp. baking soda

2 bananas, sliced thinly

2 cups plain soy milk (although you can use almond milk if you'd prefer)

2 Tbs. canola oil or low calorie butter substitute

2 tsp. egg replacement powder or egg substitute

2 tsp. fresh lemon juice

Directions

Mix together 1 ¾ cups of soy milk with the lemon juice in a bowl. Allow to stand for around five minutes. Meanwhile, combine both buckwheat and regular flour with baking powder, baking soda and salt in another bowl. Use remaining ¼ cup of soy milk to whip up the egg replacement powder in a separate bowl, and then add the mixture to the bowl of soy milk and lemon juice. Whisk in maple syrup and oil. Stir milk mixture into flour mixture. Fold in the bananas.

Lightly grease your waffle maker with cooking spray. For each waffle, pour 2 tablespoons of batter into the waffle maker, and allow to cook until they are brown (follow the instructions for your waffle maker). Serve with your favorite low calorie maple syrup, or serve plain with low calorie whipped cream and a handful of strawberries, additional frozen bananas, blueberries, or your other favorite fruit.Make sure you also check out my recipe for super yummy low calorie pancakes if you are looking for a great low calorie breakfast.

Sunday, August 22, 2010

Cool Off with a Low Calorie Fruit Popsicle

The fun days of summer continue, but so does the heat! While we all have our favorite ways to stay cool, one of my favorites is chilling with a yummy and frosty fruit popsicle. And although there are tons of popsicles out there that are worthy of trying, I have become particularly fond of Breycr's Purc Fruit Bars. Thc namc says it all. Purc fruit taste with every bite...or should that be with every lick

There are two varieties of Breyer's Pure Fruit Bars that particularly attract my taste buds. The first is basic fruit bars that contain three flavor choices - you get strawberry, raspberry and tropical flavors. Then there's the pomegranate blend bars that offer the exotic taste of pomegranate (which I love) along with blueberry, mango, or mixed berry. Talk about a sensation for your tongue! You can find these mouth-watering frozen delights packaged in twelve bar boxes or as single serve treats. And the good news is, they are available in your grocer's freezer without the need to head to a specialty foods store. Yep, gotta love the guys at Breyer's for recognizing that the health-conscious crowd is growing, and we demand flavorful but healthy treats!

These bars are low, low calorie - just 40 calories per serving with absolutely no fat, which means there's no trans-fats or saturated fats to worry about. So they are just one weight watchers point, so a perfect addition to any day. And they are cholesterol free! They contain only 9 grams of sugar per serving and provide ten percent of the RDA of Vitamin C that you need in each bar.

I have found that when I have a craving for something sweet that a Pure Fruit Bar is just what I need to feed those cravings without having to feel guilty about it later. And during these last sweltering days of summer, these bars are perfect to give to your kids without filling them full of sugary popsicles that are made with high fructose corn syrup. They won't know the difference!

Which is Better For Your Diet - Butter or Margarine

The age-old debate on which is better - margarine or butter (or could it be Parkay, like in the old commercials) rages on. If you are looking at which is better for you - from a fat and calories standpoint, the fact is that they are almost equal. Both margarine and butter are around 35 calories and 4 fat grams per teaspoon. But is one of them better for you than the other Well, sort-of. Are there other, better options out there Yes, absolutely!

About Butter

Butter is an animal product. It is high in saturated fat and dietary cholesterol. Butter in your diet can not only clog your arteries but it can also increase your risk of heart disease and deadly or debilitating stroke. It is also suggested by some research that butter can contain traces of antibiotics and hormones that are fed to animals. And even though butter is a rich source of fat-soluble vitamins like Vitamins A, D, E, and K, this one small healthful benefit, although a real one, doesn't outweigh the bad things that butter represents. In truth, the fact that people who make and sell butter would even bother to point out that butter provides you with these vitamins is akin to their grasping at straws to try to save an industry that is on the decline. You'd have to eat a lot of butter to reap any benefits from it, but by that time, your arteries would be running with pure butter....now on to margarine.

About Margarine

Ah, margarine. Butter's cousin from the 'other side of the tracks'. At first glance, margarine appears (big emphasis on the word 'appears' here) to have everything right that butter gets wrong. It is made from vegetable oil, and it is low in saturated fat and contains no dietary cholesterol. But that's where its accolades stop suddenly, especially if you are purchasing the stick margarine that is so popular these days. The process that stick margarine goes through in order to be hardened is called hydrogenation, and it is high in trans-fatty acids. Trans fat not only raises your bad cholesterol - but lowers your good cholesterol, which is your defense against artery clogging fats! Yep, trans fat can be more evil than saturated fat, it's true. So what's a girl (or guy) to do to get that delicious buttery flavor

Using Butter in your Low Calorie Diet

Enter the light spread. There are a few light spreads (and even some light margarine) on the market that is completely trans-fat free! I particularly like Promise Light Buttery Spread as a low fat butter substitute. There are also some spreads out there that contain plant stanols and sterols, which block cholesterol from being absorbed by the body. These light spreads (and some margarines) have not been hydrogenated, and are sold in tubs, not sticks.

For cooking, spreads are not ideal. Choose heart-healthy canola or olive oil instead, or better yet, opt for a low calorie cooking spray or low cal broth which will shave off additional fat and calories. When baking, try substituting low fat or fat free yogurt or low calorie sour cream, or fruit purees in recipes that call for butter or margarine; recipes like this are still delicious, they are just a bit "denser".

Arctic Zero - Low Calorie, Low Fat Ice Cream - 150 calories per PINT.

Okay, you've likely heard about having your cake and eating it too, but what about ice cream Arctic Zero is an ice cream-like treat that you can eat without guilt that is bound to cool you down quickly while satisfying your craving for ice cream!

I discovered these pint-sized ice cream treats at Whole Foods, and I was a bit hesitant to believe that someone could eat an entire pint of delicious ice cream for 150 calories. Sounds too good to be true, right Especially a product without artificial gunk in it Thinking that it would be a terrible experience, I picked up a pint of the vanilla maple Arctic Zero to give it a try anyway just to see what could possibly be in there. :) It definitely wasn't perfect rich creamy ice cream, but it really exceeded my expectations. And, when I'm in the mood for ice cream and don't have a lot of calories to spare, it is something I'm happy to reach for.

Arctic Zero is an all natural treat that is also fat free and free from gluten. This kosher treat is also perfect for those who are lactose intolerant as it is made with a high quality whey protein concentrate. And while I started my adventure with Arctic Zero with the delicious vanilla maple, I have since experimented with (and found each just as good as the other) chocolate peanut butter, and strawberry banana. According to their website, Arctic Zero also comes in mint chocolate cookie and cookies and cream which I've never had the opportunity to try.

So what's it sweetened with According to their website, research and development guys at the company were looking for more natural source of sugar when they combined organic cane sugar with monk fruit concentrate and then added eight grams of fiber to every pint. The monk fruit is known as the sweetest melon in the world, with a sweetness that is 150 times that of sugar - so just one gram of monk fruit concentrate replaces, get this, 40 teaspoons of sugar. And its free from both saturated and trans-fats...what could be better Here is the full ingredient list by the way: "Purified water, whey protein concentrate, organic cane sugar, chicory root, guar gum, xantham gum, natural flavors, sea salt, monk fruit concentrate."

Currently, you can find Arctic Zero in thirty-seven states and that number is growing, or you can order it online at Amazon. I buy it at Whole Foods which gives me confidence that nothing shady is going on. :) I'm still a bit skeptical, though.

If you are a serious ice cream addict looking for the lowest calorie ice cream out there, then this is definitely worth a try. Each pint is 150 calories, so 2 weight watchers point. Or, 1 weight watchers point per quarter pint serving.

If you are looking for something super yummy, and have a few _more_ calories to spare, I recommend you eat Julie's low calorie ice cream sandwiches or so delicious low fat mini ice cream sandwiches, so delicious vanilla ice cream bar, or low calorie frozen yogurt.

Get Your Chocolate Fix - for Just 60 Calories!

One of the biggest drawbacks for a lot of folks when it comes to sticking to a diet is avoiding chocolate. But why avoid it when you can incorporate delicious low calorie chocolate treats into your dieting plan Chuao (pronounced as chew-wow) Chocolatier is a maker of fine chocolate, and they are quickly becoming known for providing dieters around the world with a chocolate fix in the form of the Choco-Pod.

I really like Choco-Pods. They are shaped like a cacao pod (the source of the beans that are used to make chocolate) and are filled with your favorite fruit flavors, including strawberry and balsamic caramel (this is my favorite), passion fruit caramel, banana brown sugar caramel, spicy cabernet caramel, and spicy macadamia praline. I stumbled upon these at my local Whole Foods store and thought what the heck. Sixty calories and get my chocolate fix too, you can't beat that! So a new relationship was formed. And now, I've seen them popping up at other places, like my local coffee shop. So, keep your eye out if you don't have a Whole Foods.

The chocolate in Choco-Pods are made using Venezuelan chocolate and contain sixty percent cacao. In addition to the caramel flavor (I love anything low calorie caramel), I particularly like the passion fruit for its spicy yet sour flavor that blends so well with the chocolate. I am also fond of the banana brown sugar caramel - it is possibly the sweetest of them all and has the flavor of a ripe banana blended with a burnt sugar flavor that makes it exotic and unexpected.Yum!

I like the original solid Choco-Pod, too. It is available in two chocolate flavors - spicy Maya (named for the first culture that actually worshipped chocolate) which is flavored with ancient spices like cinnamon, cayenne pepper and Pasilla chile - and nutmeg, which has a subtle flavor of cardamom and nutmeg.

Each Choco-Pod is wrapped in an individual wrapper (in boxes of 12) so that you can take one with you, without having to risk eating more than one portion. They are just one weight watchers (WW) point each!

Chapter 5

Organic Food, Health and Tourism

To start with, they exclude all the foreign materials added to traditional foods which tend to be toxic. If one practices eating organically produced foods, one is guaranteed of a better and healthier diet to sustain the human body. This is because all the nutrients, the vitamins and minerals required for the maintenance of the human body are constantly being made available. Consumption also reduces the risk at which one can get cancer which is very important. No one wants to die a painful death or at a young age and for this to be a possibility organic foods are highly recommended. Also, these foods are 90% safer in the sense that human waste or animal excretions are not being incorporated in the production. In traditional foods, it is believed that the water supplies have a percentage of human waste and animal excretions present. And it is also assumed that these two play contribute to the diseases spreading in the world today. Therefore to be on the safer side and avoid any trouble, one must rely on organically manufactured foods which do not have any of these materials in the water supply. The water is a hundred percent pure because it is tested in labs to ensure its purity.

The Living Soil Association of Tasmania (1946-1960) was founded in Hobart, Tasmania on 30 August 1946. It was one of the world's first advocacy groups for organic farming. The Living Soil Association of Tasmania affiliated with the Australian Organic Farming and Gardening Society (founded 4 October 1944) and the UK's Soil Association (founded 3 May 1946).

The Living Soil Association of Tasmania distributed to its members the quarterly journal of the Australian Organic Farming and Gardening Society, the Organic Farming Digest, which later became the 'Farming & Gardening Digest incorporating the Organic Farming Digest'. The Association also produced six issues of its own Newsletter and a booklet 'Compost - How and Why'.

The founder and president of the Living Soil Association of Tasmania' was Henry Shoobridge (1874-1963), a local successful hop grower , and accredited Methodist preacher.

The Living Soil Association of Tasmania was successful in recruiting 11 representatives of government and other associations onto its Council. These included the Education Department of Tasmania, the Hobart City Council, the Tasmanian Farmers Federation and the Tasmanian Farmers Stockowners and Orchardists Association. Included in the Rules & Constitution of the Living Soil Association of Tasmania was the provision for Junior Groups. Membership of the Living Soil Association of Tasmania peaked in 1952. There is no trace of the Association after 1960. Another thing is that organic foods supports the environmentally friendly cause in that it doesn't allow the secretion of harmful materials into the atmosphere and ultimately the environment. Pesticides and herbicides used in traditionally produced foods are harmful to the environment especially to aquatic organisms. Therefore organic foods encourage the cause to make the environment a safer place to live in and help in improving the environment.

Finally, these foods don't result in the emission of green house gases which affect and unstabilize the atmospheric conditions.

If ponders over it, it's amazing that organic foods are expensive. Why should it be For the fact that they no added supplements it makes it difficult to understand why they should be expensive. However, little facts when looked at will explain why organic foods are expensive.

First of all, these foods are limited in quantity. Production is lesser than traditional foods because of the time it takes for them to grow. Hormones which are added to traditional foods speed up growth of foods. This material and in fact other foreign materials are not included in organic foods meaning that the foods grown organically will use the full cycle they need to grow. This therefore reduces the number of organically grown foods on the market.

With the low number of organic foods and the high demand for them on the market the prices hitch up. Here the laws of economics are put into play. Where sellers see that a product is high in demand and the amount is low, they will increase the prices because they know that buyers are willing to pay anything to buy quality products.

Additionally, the prices of these foods increase because of the stages it passes through before getting on the market. On the production side, the cost of production forces the price to be raised. Then in the processing unit, the cost involved increases the price further. Then it goes through the harvesting section where process involves incurs an extra cost. Then the transportation from place of production to marketplaces increases the price even further. Finally at the marketing place, the sellers add to the already increased price to make profit from their business. Hence, the product's price has increased dramatically considering the stages it passes through.

The Australian Organic Farming and Gardening Society (1944-1955) was founded in Sydney on 5 October 1944, during the closing months of World War II. It came into being two years before the United Kingdom's Soil Association, thus becoming the first agriculture organisation in the world to call itself an "organic" association.

The Australian Organic Farming and Gardening Society produced a quarterly journal, Organic Farming

Digest (1946-1954), which was the first "organic" journal to be published by an association. The Digest published Australian, British, American, European and African authors. About half the articles published were written by Australians.

The primary Australian authors were V. H. Kelly and New South Wales grazier, Colonel Harold White. The main UK authors were Albert Howard and F. C. King, and the main U.S. authors published in Organic Farming Digest were Ehrenfried Pfeiffer and J. I. Rodale.

For a decade, the Society promoted organic agriculture throughout Australia and beyond, but ultimately disbanded on 19 January 1955, with lack of funds given as the reason.

This goes a long way to showing that things that are good for the human body do not come cheap but come at an extra cost that one has to be willing to pay for.

Organic Foods helps in reducing the probability of getting cancer. It sounds unbelievable but this is true and has been scientifically proved over and over again. One may ask how, well it is simple. Organic foods increase the antioxidant level in the body. Antioxidants are essential in eliminating the chances of getting cancer as one grows older. Now, someone might be wondering what antioxidants are and the relationship it has with organic foods. To answer that question, "antioxidants are compounds that may shield cells from the impairment initiated by unstable substances that are known as free radicals. Free radical impairment is the main reason behind the cause of cancer. Antioxidants merge with and cause the free radicals to stabilize and may stop some of the impairment free radicals might then cause" (Source: National Cancer Institute).

With antioxidants understood, one can clearly see why they are important for the human system especially as we grow older and our immune system cannot combat certain bodily reactions. To further open the eyes of people on the benefits of organic foods, it must be observed that traditional foods make use of pesticides, herbicides and hormones which contribute largely to cancer development. Imagine increasing your chances of getting a disease which can kill when eating food which is meant for survival.

It is better to prevent than to neglect an impending situation. To stick on the safer side, the population should encourage organic food consumption for good health and in the long run reduction in the death rates.

Cancer, "which is any malignant growth or tumor caused by abnormal and uncontrolled cell division" (Source: Princeton University, WordNet) can therefore be easily combated by organic foods. This is simply because the more organic foods a person take the higher the quantity of antioxidants in that person system and this therefore provides a higher percentage of the body's system in fighting off unstable growths and stabilizing these molecules.

Organic foods which guarantee nutritional requirements in a person's diet are becoming increasingly popular in many parts of the world. With more and more people being concerned about what they take in to check their health, organic foods have increasingly become the number one option amongst many shoppers. It is now being found in major supermarkets and these trends tell us that this food is here to stay. Many have their doubts about it. However one must realize that when traditional foods are compared to organic foods, the facts favor organic foods more.

First of all, organic foods are produced naturally without anything foreign included but traditional foods are constantly sprayed with pesticides, herbicides, hormones and many other chemicals. Imagine eating foodstuffs which have a certain percentage of foreign materials, many of which tend to be dangerously poisonous. Even with that aside, these things can have harmful effects on the environment and the human body as well. With this settled, any individual would clearly go in for organic foods which guarantees nutritional intake and no foreign materials.

With this agreed on, one may wonder how this will affect the future but it does. A person who takes in organically produced foods and knows of its benefits will feed his/her children on it. If this family grows on organic food, the trend will not stay there but will be transferred from family to family and generation to generation into the future.

Who said the future of organically produced foods is bleak. Do you know that in the developing world an organic foods farmer earns more than a traditional foods farmer They have higher standard of living. Who doesn't want that If that is the source of income for a family then all signs go a long way to showing that organic foods will increasingly become popular in the future.

In spite of all the benefits that organic food provides, some people feel that it is costlier as compared to other non organic foods. Even though it may be slightly costlier, because of the immense benefits that it is providing it can be safely said that it is better than non organic food. But still if you want the cost of organic food to come down, then you can buy organic food in bulk. If you are looking to buy organic food in bulk then the price of organic food comes down immensely.

Buying food in bulk will lower your costs and also ensure that you have enough of organic food for yourself and your family and hence you will not have to make frequent trips to the organic food store. Hence buying organic food in bulk will prove to be a better option for all health lovers. If you want to know where you can get organic food in bulk in your area you can simply run a google search on the internet. You can also contact one of the below mentioned organic food stores in order to buy organic food in bulk. These stores are known to provide fresh organic food in large quantities at decent prices hence satisfying all your needs.

Organic foods are made in a way that limits the use of synthetic materials during production. For the vast majority of human history, agriculture can be described as organic; only during the 20th century was a large supply of new synthetic chemicals introduced to the food supply. This more recent style of production is referred to as "conventional." Under organic production, the use of conventional non-organic pesticides, insecticides and herbicides is greatly restricted and saved as a last resort. However, contrary to popular belief, certain non-organic fertilizers are still used. If livestock are involved, they must be reared without the routine use of antibiotics and without the use of growth hormones, and generally fed a healthy diet. In most countries, organic produce may not be genetically modified. It has been suggested that the application of nanotechnology to food and agriculture is a further technology that needs to be excluded from certified organic food. The Soil Association (UK) has been the first organic certifier to implement a nano-exclusion.

Organic food production is a heavily regulated industry, distinct from private gardening. Currently, the European Union, the United States, Canada, Japan and many other countries require producers to obtain special certification in order to market food as "organic" within their borders. Most certifications allow some chemicals and pesticides to be used, so consumers should be aware of the standards for qualifying as "organic" in their respective locales.

Historically, organic farms have been relatively small family-run operations, which is why organic food was once only available in small stores or farmers' markets. However, since the early 1990s organic food production has had growth rates of around 20% a year, far ahead of the rest of the food industry, in both developed and developing nations. As of April 2008, organic food accounts for 1-2% of food sales worldwide.

In 1939, Lord Northbourne coined the term organic farming in his book Look to the Land (1940), out of his conception of "the farm as organism," to describe a holistic, ecologically-balanced approach to farming-in contrast to what he called chemical farming, which relied on "imported fertility" and "cannot be self-sufficient nor an organic whole." This is different from the scientific use of the term "organic," to refer to a class of molecules that contain carbon, especially those involved in the chemistry of life.

IDENTIFYING ORGANIC FOOD

Processed organic food usually contains only organic ingredients. If non-organic ingredients are present, at least a certain percentage of the food's total plant and animal ingredients must be organic (95% in the United States, Canada, and Australia) and any non-organically produced ingredients are subject to various agricultural requirements. Foods claiming to be organic must be free of artificial food additives, and are often processed with fewer artificial methods, materials and conditions, such as chemical ripening, food irradiation, and genetically modified ingredients. Pesticides are allowed so long as they are not synthetic.

Early consumers interested in organic food would look for non-chemically treated,non-use of unapproved pesticides, fresh or minimally processed food. They mostly had to buy directly from growers: "Know your farmer, know your food" was the motto. Personal definitions of what constituted "organic" were developed through firsthand experience: by talking to farmers, seeing farm conditions, and farming activities. Small farms grew vegetables (and raised livestock) using organic farming practices, with or without certification, and the individual consumer monitored. As demand for organic foods continued to increase, high volume sales through mass outlets such as supermarkets rapidly replaced the direct farmer connection. Today there is no limit to organic farm sizes and many large corporate farms currently have an organic division. However, for supermarket consumers, food production is not easily observable, and product labeling, like "certified organic", is relied on. Government regulations and third-party inspectors are looked to for assurance.

The USDA carries out routine inspections of farms that produce USDA Organic labeled foods. Of the 30 third party inspectors 15 of them have been placed under probation after an audit. On April 20, 2010, the Department of Agriculture said that it would begin enforcing rules requiring the spot testing of organically grown foods for traces of pesticides, after an auditor exposed major gaps in federal oversight of the organic food industry.

Legal Definition

The National Organic Program (run by the USDA) is in charge of the legal definition of organic in the United States and does organic certification.

To be certified organic, products must be grown and manufactured in a manner that adheres to standards set by the country they are sold in:

- Australia: Australian Organic Standard and NASAA Organic Standard
- Canada: Canada Gazette, Government of Canada
- European Union: EU-Eco-regulation

  Sweden: KRAV

  United Kingdom: Department for Environment, Food and Rural Affairs (DEFRA)
- Norway: Debio Organic certification
- India: NPOP, (National Program for Organic Production)
- Japan: JAS Standards.
- United States: National Organic Program (NOP) Standards

Environmental Impact

Several surveys and studies have attempted to examine and compare conventional and organic systems of farming. The general consensus across these surveys is that organic farming is less damaging for the following reasons:

- Organic farms do not consume or release synthetic pesticides into the environment-some of which have the potential to harm soil, water and local terrestrial and aquatic wildlife.
- Organic farms are better than conventional farms at sustaining diverse ecosystems, i.e., populations of plants and insects, as well as animals.

- When calculated either per unit area or per unit of yield, organic farms use less energy and produce less waste, e.g., waste such as packaging materials for chemicals.

However, some critics of organic farming methods believe that organic farms require more land to produce the same amount of food as conventional farms (see 'Yield' section, below). They argue that if this is true, organic farms could potentially destroy the rain forests and wipe out many ecosystems.

A 2003 investigation by the Department for Environment Food and Rural Affairs in the UK found, similar to other reports, that organic farming "can produce positive environmental benefits", but that some of the benefits were decreased or lost when comparisons are made on "the basis of unit production rather than area".

Yield

One study found a 20% smaller yield from organic farms using 50% less fertilizer and 97% less pesticide. Studies comparing yields have had mixed results. Supporters claim that organically managed soil has a higher quality and higher water retention. This may help increase yields for organic farms in drought years.

One study from the Danish Environmental Protection Agency found that, area-for-area, organic farms of potatoes, sugar beet and seed grass produce as little as half the output of conventional farming. Findings like these, and the dependence of organic food on manure from low-yield cattle, has prompted criticism from scientists that organic farming is environmentally unsound and incapable of feeding the world population. Among these critics are Norman Borlaug, father of the "green revolution," and winner of the Nobel Peace Prize, who asserts that organic farming practices can at most feed 4 billion people, after expanding cropland dramatically and destroying ecosystems in the process. Michael Pollan, author of The Omnivore's Dilemma, responds to this by pointing out that the average yield of world agriculture is substantially lower than modern sustainable farming yields. Bringing average world yields up to modern organic levels could increase the worlds food supply by 50 %.

A 2007 study compiling research from 293 different comparisons into a single study to assess the overall efficiency of the two agricultural systems has concluded that...organic methods could produce enough food on a global per capita basis to sustain the current human population, and potentially an even larger population, without increasing the agricultural land base.

The researchers also found that while in developed countries, organic systems on average produce 92% of the yield produced by conventional agriculture, organic systems produce 80% more than conventional farms in developing countries, because the materials needed for organic farming are more accessible than synthetic farming materials to farmers in some poor countries. On the other hand, communities that lack sufficient manure to replenish soils would struggle with organic farming, and the soil would degrade rapidly.

Energy Efficiency

A study of the sustainability of apple production systems showed that in comparing a conventional farming system to an organic method of farming, the organic system is more energy efficient. However, this is debatable due to organic farming's large use of tillage for weed control. Also increased fuel use from incorporating less nutrient dense fertilizers results in higher fuel consumption rates. The general analysis is that organic production methods are usually more energy efficient because they do not use chemically synthesized nitrogen. But they generally consume more petroleum because of the lack of other options for weed control and more intensive soil management practices.

Energy efficiency is hard to determine; in the case listed above the author cites a book written in 1976. The true value of efficiency and energy consumption in relation to organic farms has yet to be determined.

Pesticides and Farmers

There are studies detailing the effects and side effects of pesticides upon the health of farm workers. Even when pesticides are used correctly, they still end up in the air and bodies of farm workers. Through these studies, organophosphate pesticides have become associated with acute health problems such as abdominal pain, dizziness, headaches, nausea, vomiting, as well as skin and eye problems. In addition, there have been many other studies that have found pesticide exposure is associated with more severe health problems such as respiratory problems, memory disorders, dermatologic conditions, cancer, depression, neurologic deficits, miscarriages, and birth defects. Summaries of peer-reviewed research have examined the link between pesticide exposure and neurological outcomes and cancer in organophosphate-exposed workers. Those pesticides found to cause major health problems are banned for use in agriculture, conventional or organic, in many developed counties.

Imported fruits and vegetables from South America are more likely to contain high level of pesticides, even pesticides banned for use in the United States. Migratory birds, such as Swainson's hawks, have wintering grounds in Argentina where thousands of them were found dead from monocrotophos insecticide poisoning.

Pesticide residue

A study published in 2002 showed that "Organically grown foods consistently had about one-third as many residues as conventionally grown foods."

Monitoring of pesticide residues in the United States is carried out by the Pesticide Data Program, a branch of the USDA created in 1990. It has since tested over 60 different types of food for over 400 different types of pesticides - with samples collected close to the point of consumption. Their most recent results found in 2005 that:

" These data indicate that 29.5 percent of all samples tested contained no detectable pesticides [parent compound and metabolite(s) combined], 30 percent contained 1 pesticide, and slightly over 40 percent contained more than 1 pesticide."

-USDA, Pesticide Data Program

Several studies corroborate this finding by having found that 25 percent of organic food carries synthetic pesticide residues, in comparison to 77 percent of conventional food.

Safety and Pesticides

A study published by the National Research Council in 1993 determined that for infants and children, the major source of exposure to pesticides is through diet. A recent study in 2006 measured the levels of organophosphorus pesticide exposure in 23 schoolchildren before and after replacing their diet with organic food. In this study it was found that levels of organophosphorus pesticide exposure dropped dramatically and immediately when the children switched to an organic diet. Food residue limits established by law are set specifically with children in mind and consider a child's lifetime ingestion of each pesticide.

There are controversial data on the health implications of certain pesticides. For example, the herbicide Atrazine has been shown in some experiments to be a teratogen, causing demasculinization in male frogs exposed to small concentrations. Under the effects of Atrazine, male frogs were found to have greatly increased occurrences of either malformed gonads, or testicular gonads which contain non-degenerate eggs. Effects were however significantly reduced in high concentrations, as is consistent with other teratogens affecting the endocrine system, such as estradiol.

Organic farming standards do not allow the use of synthetic pesticides, but they do allow the use of specific pesticides derived from plants. The most common organic pesticides, accepted for restricted use by most organic standards, include Bt, pyrethrum and rotenone. Rotenone has high toxicity to fish and aquatic creatures, causes Parkinson's disease if injected into rats, and shows other toxicity to mammals.

The United States Environmental Protection Agency and state agencies periodically review the licensing of suspect pesticides, but the process of de-listing is slow. One example of this slow process is exemplified by the pesticide Dichlorvos, or DDVP, which as recently as the year 2006 the EPA proposed its continued sale. The EPA has almost banned this pesticide on several occasions since the 1970s, but it never did so despite considerable evidence that suggests DDVP is not only carcinogenic but dangerous to the human nervous system-especially in children. The EPA "has determined that risks do not exceed levels of concern", a study of longterm exposure to DDVP in rats showed no toxic effects.

Nutritional Value and Taste

In April 2009, results from Quality Low Input Food, a 5-year integrated study funded by the European Commission, confirmed that "the quality of crops and livestock products from organic and conventional farming systems differs considerably." Specifically, results from a QLIF project studying the effects of organic and low-input farming on crop and livestock nutritional quality "showed that organic food production methods resulted in some case: (a) higher levels of nutritionally desirable compounds (e.g., vitamins/antioxidants and poly-unsaturated fatty acids such as omega-3 and CLA); (b) lower levels of nutritionally undesirable compounds such as heavy metals, mycotoxins, pesticide residues and glyco-alkaloids in a range of crops and/or milk; (c) a lower risk of faecal Salmonella shedding in pigs." but also showed no significant difference between traditionally grown foods on other studies. The QLIF study also concludes that "further and more detailed studies are required to provide proof for positive health impacts of organic diets on human and animal health." Alternatively, according to the UK's Food Standards Agency, "Consumers may choose to buy organic fruit, vegetables and meat because they believe them to be more nutritious than other food. However, the balance of current scientific evidence does not support this view." A 12-month systematic review commissioned by the FSA in 2009 and conducted at the London School of Hygiene & Tropical Medicine based on 50 years' worth of collected evidence concluded that "there is no good evidence that consumption of organic food is beneficial to health in relation to nutrient content." Other studies have found no proof that organic food offers greater nutritional values, more consumer safety or any distinguishable difference in taste.

Regarding taste, a 2001 study concluded that organic apples were sweeter by blind taste test. Firmness of the apples was also rated higher than those grown conventionally. Limited use of food preservatives may cause faster spoilage of organic foods. Organic food may also potentially have higher amounts of natural biotoxins, like solanine in potatoes, as to compensate for the lack of externally applied fungicides and herbicides etc. However, in current studies, there have been no indications of difference in amounts of natural biotoxins between organic and conventional foods.

Cost

Organic products typically cost 10 to 40% more than similar conventionally produced products. According to the USDA, Americans, on average, spent $1,347 on groceries in 2004; thus switching entirely to organics would raise their cost of groceries by $538.80 per year ($44.90/month) and switching to half organics would raise costs by $269.40 ($22.45/month). Processed organic foods vary in price when compared to their conventional counterparts. An Australian study by Choice magazine in 2004 found processed organic foods in supermarkets to be 65% more expensive, but noted this was not consistent. Prices may be higher because organic produce is produced on a smaller scale, and may need to be milled or processed separately. Furthermore, there is an increase in shipping costs from more centralized production in otherwise regional markets. In the case of dairy and eggs, the animal's requirements such as the number of animals that can be raised per acre, or the breed of animal and its feed conversion ratio affects the costs.

Related Movements

Biodynamic agriculture, a method of organic farming, is closely related to the organic food movement.

Food Co-ops and buyers groups are alternative ways of selling food which have also been closely related to the organic food movement. These co-operative structures have been aimed at lowering the retail price of organic food and some attempt to reducc the food miles associated with the produce.

While organic food accounts for 1-2% of total food sales worldwide, the organic food market is growing rapidly, far ahead of the rest of the food industry, in both developed and developing nations.

- World organic food sales jumped from US $23 billion in 2002 to $52 billion in 2008.
- The world organic market has been growing by 20% a year since the early 1990s, with future growth estimates ranging from 10%-50% annually depending on the country.

North America

United States:

- Organic food is the fastest growing sector of the American food marketplace.

- Organic food sales have grown by 17 to 20 percent a year for the past few years while sales of conventional food have grown at only about 2 to 3 percent a year.
- In 2003 organic products were available in nearly 20,000 natural food stores and 73% of conventional grocery stores.
- Organic products account for 2.6% of total food sales in the year 2005.
- Two thirds of organic milk and cream and half of organic cheese and yogurt are sold through conventional supermarkets.

Canada:

- Organic food sales surpassed $1 billion in 2006, accounting for 0.9% of food sales in Canada.
- Organic food sales by grocery stores were 28% higher in 2006 than in 2005.
- British Columbians account for 13% of the Canadian population, but purchased 26% of the organic food sold in Canada in 2006.

EUROPE

In the European Union (EU25) 3.9% of the total utilized agricultural area is used for organic production. The countries with the highest proportion of organic land are Austria (11%) and Italy (8.4), followed by Czech Republic and Greece (both 7.2%). The lowest figures are shown for Malta (0.1%), Poland (0.6%) and Ireland (0.8%)

AUSTRIA

- 11.6% of all farmers produced organically in 2007. The government has created incentives to increase the figure to 20% by 2010.
- 4.9% of all food products sold in Austrian supermarkets (including discount stores) in 2006 were organic. 8000 different organic products were available in the same year.

Italy

- Since 2000 use of some organic food is compulsory in Italian schools and hospitals. Since 2005 all school lunches in Emilia Romagna must be organic by law.

Poland

- In 2005 168,000 ha of land were under organic management. 7 percent of Polish consumers buy food that was produced according to the EU-Eco-regulation. The value of the organic market is estimated at 50 million Euros (2006).

UK

- Organic food sales increased from just over £100 million in 1993/94 to £1.21 billion in 2004 (an 11% increase on 2003).

Caribbean

Cuba

After the collapse of the Soviet Union in 1990, agricultural inputs that had previously been purchased from Eastern bloc countries were no longer available in Cuba, and many Cuban farms converted to organic methods out of necessity. Consequently, organic agriculture is a mainstream practice in Cuba, while it remains an alternative practice in most other countries. Although some products called organic in Cuba would not satisfy certification requirements in other countries (crops may be genetically modified, for example), Cuba exports organic citrus and citrus juices to EU markets that meet EU organic standards. Cuba's forced conversion to organic methods may position the country to be a global supplier of organic products.

Organic farming is the form of agriculture that relies on techniques such as crop rotation, green manure, compost, and biological pest control, to maintain soil productivity and control pests on a farm. Organic farming excludes or strictly limits the use of synthetic fertilizers and synthetic pesticides, plant growth regulators, livestock antibiotics, food additives, and genetically modified organisms.

Organic agricultural methods are internationally regulated and legally enforced by many nations, based in large part on the standards set by the International Federation of Organic Agriculture Movements (IFOAM), an international umbrella organization for organic organizations established in 1972. IFOAM defines the overarching goal of organic farming as follows:

"Organic agriculture is a production system that sustains the health of soils, ecosystems and people. It relies on ecological processes, biodiversity and cycles adapted to local conditions, rather than the use of inputs with adverse effects. Organic agriculture combines tradition, innovation and science to benefit the shared environment and promote fair relationships and a good quality of life for all involved.."

-International Federation of Organic Agriculture Movements.

Since 1990, the market for organic products has grown at a rapid pace, to reach $46 billion in 2007. This demand has driven a similar increase in organically managed farmland. Approximately 32.2 million hectares worldwide are now farmed organically, representing approximately 0.8 percent of total world farmland. In addition, as of 2007 organic wild products are harvested on approximately 30 million hectares.

The organic movement began in the 1930s and 1940s as a reaction to agriculture's growing reliance on synthetic fertilizers. Artificial fertilizers had been created during the 18th century, initially with superphosphates and then ammonia derived fertilizers mass-produced using the Haber-Bosch process developed during World War I. These early fertilizers were cheap, powerful, and easy to transport in bulk. Similar advances occurred in chemical pesticides in the 1940s, leading to the decade being referred to as the 'pesticide era'.

Sir Albert Howard is widely considered to be the father of organic farming. Further work was done by J.I. Rodale in the United States, Lady Eve Balfour in the United Kingdom, and many others across the world.

As a percentage of total agricultural output, organic farming has remained tiny since its beginning. As environmental awareness and concern increased amongst the general population, the originally supply-driven movement became demand-driven. Premium prices from consumers and in some cases government subsidies attracted many farmers into converting. In the developing world, many farmers farm according to traditional methods which are comparable to organic farming but are not certified. In other cases, farmers in the developing world have converted for economic reasons. As a proportion of total global agricultural output, organic output remains small, but it has been growing rapidly in many countries, notably in Europe.

Methods

Organic cultivation of mixed vegetables in Capay, California. Note the hedgerow in the background.

"An organic farm, properly speaking, is not one that uses certain methods and substances and avoids others; it is a farm whose structure is formed in imitation of the structure of a natural system that has the integrity, the independence and the benign dependence of an organism"

-Wendell Berry, "The Gift of Good Land"

Soil Management

Plants need nitrogen, phosphorus, and potassium, as well as micronutrients and symbiotic relationships with fungi and other organisms to flourish, but getting enough nitrogen, and particularly synchronization so that plants get enough nitrogen at the right time (when plants need it most), is likely the greatest challenge for organic farmers. Crop rotation and green manure ("cover crops") help to provide nitrogen through legumes (more precisely, the Fabaceae family) which fix nitrogen from the atmosphere through symbiosis with the bacteria rhizobia. Intercropping, which is sometimes used for insect and disease control, can also increase soil nutrients, but the competition between the legume and the crop can be problematic and wider spacing between crop rows is required. Crop residues can be ploughed back into the soil, and different plants leave different amounts of nitrogen, potentially aiding synchronization. Organic farmers also use animal manure, certain processed fertilizers such as seed meal and various mineral powders such as rock phosphate and greensand, a naturally occurring form of potash which provides potassium. Altogether these methods help to control erosion. In some cases pH may need to be amended. Natural pH amendments include lime and sulfur, but in the U.S. some synthetic compounds such as iron sulfate, aluminum sulfate, magnesium sulfate, and soluble boron products are allowed in organic farming.

Mixed farms with both livestock and crops can operate as ley farms, whereby the land gathers fertility through growing nitrogen-fixing forage grasses such as white clover or alfalfa and grows cash crops or cereals when fertility is established. Farms without livestock ("stockless") may find it more difficult to maintain fertility, and may rely more on external inputs such as imported manure as well as grain legumes and green manures, although grain legumes may fix limited nitrogen because they are harvested. Horticultural farms growing fruits and vegetables which operate in protected conditions are often even more reliant upon external inputs.

Weed Control

After nutrient supply, weed control is the second priority for farmers. Techniques for controlling weeds have varying levels of effectiveness and include handweeding, mulch, corn gluten meal, a natural preemergence herbicide, flame, garlic and clove oil, borax, pelargonic acid, solarization (which involves spreading clear plastic across the ground in hot weather for 4-6 weeks), vinegar, various other homemade remedies, and raise beds.:45-65 One recent innovation in rice farming is to introduce ducks and fish to wet paddy fields, which eat both weeds and insects. Raise beds are made of 2X10 untreated wood. Every raised bed acts as a composting unit. There is no need for a composting area saving space. Each raise bed is surrounded by wood chips or bricks that create an outside barrier to weeds that tend to grow from outside garden areas. The new raised beds which are filled with fresh compost (i.e. from recycling centers) are initially free from weed seeds. Weeds that may eventually appear from air born contact are easily removed from loose composted bed. Weeding only has to be done initially until plants are fully grown. Plants should have been planted close enough together that little light is available for weeds to grow, once they are fully grown in raise bed. This is opposed to older row style planting that creates open area's in field for weeds to get a foot hold in. For older raised beds that are being replanted, a layer of news paper, straw, and hay can be used to starve weeds of light composting the weeds. The weeds will be composted by the time the news paper, hay, straw breaks down. Plants that are added on top of compost will be able to easily grow through news paper, hay, straw layers.

Controlling Other Organisms

Organisms aside from weeds which cause problems include arthropods (e.g. insects, mites) and nematodes. Fungi and bacteria can cause disease.

Insect pests are a common problem, and insecticides, both non-organic and organic, are controversial due to their environmental and health effects. One way to manage insects is to ignore them and focus on plant health, since plants can survive the loss of about a third of leaf area before suffering severe growth consequences.:67 To avoid using insecticides, one can select naturally resistant plants, put bags around the plants, remove dying material such as leaves, fruit, and diseased plants, covering plants with a solid barrier ("row cover"), hosing, encouraging and releasing beneficial organisms and beneficial insects, planting companion plants and polycultures, various traps, sticky cards (which can also be used to assess insect prevalence), and season extension. Biological pest control uses natural predators to control pests. Recommended beneficial insects include minute pirate bugs, big-eyed bugs, and to a lesser extent ladybugs (which tend to fly away), all of which eat a wide range of pests. Lacewings are also effective, but tend to fly away. Praying mantis tend to move slower and eat less heavily. Parasitoid wasps tend to be effective for their selected prey, but like all small insects can be less effective outdoors because the wind controls their movement. Predatory mites are effective for controlling mites.

Several pesticides approved for organic use have been called green pesticides such as spinosad and neem. Generally, but not necessarily, organic pesticides are safer and more environmentally friendly than synthetic pesticides.:92[unreliable source] The main organic insecticides used in the US are Bt (a bacterial toxin) and pyrethrum. Surveys have found that fewer than 10% of organic farmers use these pesticides regularly; one survey found that only 5.3% of vegetable growers in California use rotenone while 1.7% use pyrethrum (Lotter 2003:26). Rotenone used to be used by some organic growers in the US, however since 2005 it has not been approved by National Organic Program guidelines. Nicotine sulfate may also be used; although it breaks down quickly, it is extremely toxic, nearly as toxic as aldicarb.:104 Less toxic but still effective organic insecticides include neem, spinosad, soaps, garlic, citrus oil, capsaicin (repellent), Bacillus popillae, Beauvaria bassiana, and boric acid.:110 Pesticides should be rotated to minimize pest resistance.

The first disease control strategy involves keeping the area clean by removing diseased and dying plants and ensure that the plants are healthy by maintaining water and fertilization.:129 Compost tea is sometimes promoted and can be effective, but there is concern over whether these are ineffective or even harmful when not made correctly. Polyculture and crop rotation reduce the ability of disease to spread. Disease-resistant cultivars can be purchased. Organic fungicides include the bacteria Bacillus subtilis, Bacillus pumilus, and Trichoderma harzianum which are mainly effective for diseases affecting roots. Bordeaux mixture contains copper, which can be used as an organic fungicide in various forms. Sulfur is effective against fungus as well as some insects. Lime sulfur is also available, but can damage plants if not used correctly. Potassium and sodium bicarbonate are also effective against fungus. Agricultural Research Service scientists also have found that caprylic acid, a naturally-occurring fatty acid in milk and coconuts, as well as other natural plant extracts have antimicrobial characteristics that can be used in the organic farming industry.

Standards

Standards regulate production methods and in some cases final output for organic agriculture. Standards may be voluntary or legislated. As early as the 1970s organic producers could be voluntarily certified by private associations. In the 1980s, governments began to produce organic production guidelines. Beginning in the 1990s, a trend toward legislation of standards began, most notably with the 1991 EU-Eco-regulation developed for European Union, which set standards for 12 countries, and a 1993 UK program. The EU's program was followed by a Japan program in 2001, and in 2002 the United States created the National Organic Program (NOP). As of 2007 over 60 countries have regulations on organic farming (IFOAM 2007:11). In 2005 IFOAM created the Principles of Organic Agriculture, an international guideline for certification criteria. Typically the agencies do not certify individual farms, but rather accredit certification groups.

Materials used in organic production and foods are tested independently by the Organic Materials Review Institute.

Composting

Under USDA organic standards, manure must be subjected to proper thermophilic composting and allowed to reach a sterilizing temperature. If raw animal manure is used, 120 days must pass before the crop is harvested if the final product comes into direct contact with the soil. For products which do not come into direct contact with soil, 90 days must pass prior to harvest.

Economics

The economics of organic farming, a subfield of agricultural economics, encompasses the entire process and effects of organic farming in terms of human society, including social costs, opportunity costs, unintended consequences, information asymmetries, and economies of scale. Although the scope of economics is broad, agricultural economics tends to focus on maximizing yields and efficiency at the farm level. Mainstream economics takes an anthropocentric approach to the value of the natural world: biodiversity, for example, is considered beneficial only to the extent that it is valued by people and increases profits. Some governments such as the European Union subsidize organic farming, in large part because these countries believe in the external benefits of reduced water use, reduced water contamination by pesticides and nutrients of organic farming, reduced soil erosion, reduced carbon emissions, increased biodiversity, and assorted other benefits.

Organic farming is labor and knowledge-intensive whereas conventional farming is capital-intensive, requiring more energy and manufactured inputs. Organic farmers in California have cited marketing as their greatest obstacle.

Geographic Producer Distribution

The markets for organic products are strongest in North America and Europe, which as of 2001 are estimated to have $6 and $8 billion respectively of the $20 billion market (2003:6). However, as of 2007 organic farmland is distributed across the globe. Australasia has 39% of the total organic farmland with Australia's 11.8 million hectares, but 97 percent of this land is sprawling rangeland (2007:35), which results in total sales of approximately 5% of US sales (2003:7). Europe has 23 percent of total organic farmland (6.9 million hectares), followed by Latin America with 19 percent (5.8 million hectares). Asia has 9.5 percent while North America has 7.2 percent. Africa has a mere 3 percent. See also Organic farming by country.

Besides Australia, the countries with the most organic area are Argentina (3.1 million hectares), China (2.3 million hectares), and the United States (1.6 million hectares). Much of Argentina's organic farmland is pasture, like that of Australia (2007:42). Italy, Spain, Germany, Brazil, Uruguay, and the UK follow the United States by the amount of land managed organically (2007:26).

Growth

As of 2001, the estimated total market value of certified organic products was estimated to be $20 billion. By 2002 this was $23 billion and by 2007 more than $46 billion according to Organic Monitor (Willer/Kilcher 2009).

In recent years both Europe (2007: 7.8 million hectares/European Union: 7.2 million hectares) and North America (2007: 2.2 million hectares) have experienced strong growth in organic farmland. However, this growth has occurred under different conditions. While the European Union has shifted agricultural subsidies to organic farmers due to perceived environmental benefits, the United States has taken a free market approach. Yet, the United States has not taken a free-market approach concerning the subsidizing of major commercial crops such as non-organic corn. As a result of this difference in policy between the US and EU, as of 2008 4.1% percent of the European Union's farmland was organically managed compared to just 0.6 percent of United States farmland (Willer/Kilcher 2009). The growth of organic farmland area in the EU was 21% from 2005 to 2008 reaching a total of 7.8 million hectares.

IFOAM's most recent edition of The World of Organic Agriculture: Statistics and Emerging Trends 2009 lists the countries which had the most hectares in 2007. The country with the most organic land is Australia with more than 12 million hectares, followed by Argentina, Brasil and the US. In total 32.2 million hectares were under organic management in 2007. For 1999 11 million hectares of organically managed land are reported (Willer/Kilcher 2009).

In recent years organic agriculture has grown tremendously. Considering this rapid growth, it is within the nature of organic farming to keep it from becoming a large scale industrial business as conventional farming has become (Duram 183). Duram, Leslie. Good Growing. Santa Cruz: Bison Books, 2005.

Productivity and Profitability

A 2006 study suggests that converted organic farms have lower pre-harvest yields than their conventional counterparts in developed countries (92%) and that organic farms have higher pre-harvest yields than their low-intensity counterparts in developing countries (132%). The researcher attributes this to a relative lack of expensive fertilizers and pesticides in the developing world compared to the intensive, subsidy-driven farming of the developed world. Nonetheless, the researcher purposely avoids making the claim that organic methods routinely outperform green-revolution (conventional) methods. This study incorporated a 1990 review of 205 crop comparisons which found that organic crops had 91% of conventional yields. A major US survey published in 2001, analyzed results from 150 growing seasons for various crops and concluded that organic yields were 95-100% of conventional yields.

Lotter (2003:10) reports that repeated studies have found that organic farms withstand severe weather conditions better than conventional farms, sometimes yielding 70-90% more than conventional farms during droughts. A 22-year farm trial study by Cornell University published in 2005 concluded that organic farming produces the same corn and soybean yields as conventional methods over the long-term averages, but consumed less energy and used zero pesticides. The results were attributed to lower yields in general but higher yields during drought years. A study of 1,804 organic farms in Central America hit by Hurricane Mitch in 1998 found that the organic farms sustained the damage much better, retaining 20 to 40% more topsoil and smaller economic losses at highly significant levels than their neighbors.

On the other hand, a prominent 21-year Swiss study found an average of 20% lower organic yields over conventional, along with 50% lower expenditure on fertilizer and energy, and 97% less pesticides. A long-term study by U.S Department of Agriculture Agricultural Research Service (ARS) scientists concluded that, contrary to widespread belief, organic farming can build up soil organic matter better than conventional no-till farming, which suggests long-term yield benefits from organic farming. An 18-year study of organic methods on nutrient-depleted soil concluded that conventional methods were superior for soil fertility and yield in a cold-temperate climate, arguing that much of the benefits from organic farming are derived from imported materials which could not be regarded as "self-sustaining".

While organic farms have lower yields, organic methods require no synthetic fertilizer and pesticides. The decreased cost on those inputs, along with the premiums which consumers pay for organic produce, create higher profits for organic farmers. Organic farms have been consistently found to be as or more profitable than conventional farms with premiums included, but without premiums profitability is mixed (Lotter 2003:11). Welsh (1999) reports that organic farmers are more profitable in the drier states of the United States, likely due to their superior drought performance.

In 2008 the UN Environmental Programme (UNEP) and UN Conference on Trade and Development (UNCTAD) issued a report which stated that "organic agriculture can be more conducive to food security in Africa than most conventional production systems, and that it is more likely to be sustainable in the long-term". The report assessed 114 projects in 24 African countries, finding that "yields had more than doubled where organic, or near-organic practices had been used" and that soil fertility and drought resistance improved.

In 2009, a review concluded that organic production was more profitable in Wisconsin, when including price premiums.

Macroeconomic Impact

Organic methods often require more labor, providing rural jobs but increasing costs to urban consumers.

Motivations

Agriculture in general imposes external costs upon society through pesticides, nutrient runoff, water usage, and assorted other problems. As organic methods minimize some of these factors, organic farming is believed to impose fewer external costs upon society. A 2000 assessment of agriculture in the UK determined total external costs costs for 1996 of 2343 million British pounds or 208 pounds per hectare. A 2005 analysis of these costs in the USA concluded that cropland imposes approximately 5 to 16 billion dollars ($30 to $96 per hectare), while livestock production imposes 714 million dollars. Both studies concluded that more should be done to internalize external costs, and neither included subsidies in their analysis, but noted that subsidies also influence the cost of agriculture to society. Both focused on purely fiscal impacts. The 2000 review included reported pesticide poisonings but did not include speculative chronic effects of pesticides, and the 2004 review relied on a 1992 estimate of the total impact of pesticides.

Pesticides

Most organic farms use fewer pesticides than conventional farms, some pesticides damage the environment or with direct exposure human health. The main five pesticides used in organic farming are Bt (a bacterial toxin), pyrethrum, rotenone, copper and sulphur. Surveys have found that fewer than 10% of organic vegetable farmers use these pesticides regularly; one survey found that only 5.3% of vegetable growers in California use rotenone while 1.7% use pyrethrum (Lotter 2003:26). Reduction and elimination of chemical pesticide use is technologically challenging. and organic pesticides are often used to complement other pest control strategies.

Pesticide runoff is one of the most significant effects of pesticide use. The USDA Natural Resources Conservation Service tracks the environmental risk posed by pesticide water contamination from farms and its conclusion has been that "the Nation's pesticide policies during the last twenty six years have succeeded in reducing overall environmental risk, in spite of slight increases in area planted and weight of pesticides applied. Nevertheless, there are still areas of the country where there is no evidence of progress, and areas where risk levels for protection of drinking water, fish, algae and crustaceans remain high".

Pest resistant genetically modified crops are an alternative to pesticide use, however concerns over the safety and the long term benefits of genetically modified food, result in the genetic modification being widely opposed in the organic farming movement.

Food Quality and Safety

Organic food is widely believed by the public to be healthier than conventional food, although the research is inconclusive. Animals fed organic diets appear to have slightly better health and reproductive performance, but similar tests in humans have not been performed. In some vegetables and cereals there is a lower concentration of protein, but it is of higher-quality. Nutrients appear to be similar with the exception of a trend towards slightly higher vitamin C in organic leafy vegetables and potatoes.

Only tentative conclusions can be drawn on the relative safety of organic food. "Organic fruits and vegetables can be expected to contain fewer agrochemical residues than conventionally grown alternatives; yet, the significance of this difference is questionable". Organic food also appears to have lower nitrate concentrations, but the health impact of nitrates is debated. Both organic and conventional food are expected to have similar concentrations of persistent organic pollutants and heavy metals. Data is limited on natural plant pesticides and their health effects, as well as the relative risks from bacterial pathogens.

Concerns have been raised that the higher expense of organic food (ranging from 45 to 200%) could limit the recommended consumption of 5 servings per day of vegetables and fruits, which are known to improve health and reduce cancer regardless of whether they are organic or conventional.

Two studies have found that children fed organic diets experienced significantly lower organo-phosphorus pesticide exposure than children fed conventional diets. Although the researchers did not collect health outcome data in this study, they concluded "it is intuitive to assume that children whose diets consist of organic food items would have a lower probability of neurologic health risks". A 2010 study associated these pesticides with an increased risk for ADHD. A 2007 study found that consumption of organic milk is associated with a decrease in risk for eczema, although no comparable benefit was found for organic fruits, vegetables, or meat.

Extensive scientific research is being carried out in Switzerland at over 200 farms to determine differences in the quality of organic food products compared to conventional in addition to other tests. The FiBL Institute has been investigating the differences at over 200 farms. It states that "organic products stand out as having higher levels of secondary plant compounds and vitamin C. In the case of milk and meat, the fatty acid profile is often better from a nutritional point of view. As far as carbohydrates and minerals, organic products are no different from conventional products. However, in regard to undesirables such as nitrate and pesticide residues, organic products have a clear advantage. A £12m EU-funded investigation into the difference between organic and ordinary farming published in 2007 found that organic foods have more nutritional value. A recent study found that organically grown produce has double the flavonoids, an important antioxidant. A 2007 study found that organically grown kiwifruit had more antioxidants than conventional kiwifruit.

Clothing Quality and Safety

Recently, organic clothing has become widely available, due to both ecological concerns and personal health concerns. Although many consumers of organic clothing merely have a dislike of synthetic chemicals, a significant portion of the organic clothing market comes from those suffering from Multiple Chemical Sensitivity, a chronic medical condition characterized by symptoms that the affected person says are adverse effects from exposure to low levels of chemicals.

Ecological concerns primarily focus around pesticide use, as 16% of the world's pesticides are used in the production of cotton.

Genetically Modified Organisms

A key characteristic of organic farming is rejection of genetically engineered products, including plants and animals. On October 19, 1998, participants at IFOAM's 12th Scientific Conference issued the Mar del Plata Declaration, where more than 600 delegates from over 60 countries voted unanimously to exclude the use of genetically modified organisms in food production and agriculture. From this point, it became widely recognized that GMOs are categorically excluded from organic farming.

Although opposition to the use of any transgenic technologies in organic farming is strong, agricultural researchers Luis Herrera-Estrella and Ariel Alvarez-Morales continue to advocate integration of transgenic technologies into organic farming as the optimal means to sustainable agriculture, particularly in the developing world. Similarly, some organic farmers question the rationale behind the ban on the use of genetically engineered seed because they see it a biological technology consistent with organic principles

Although GMOs are excluded from use in organic farming, there is concern that the pollen from genetically modified crops is increasingly contaminating organic and heirloom genetics making it difficult, if not impossible, to keep these genetics from entering the organic food supply. International trade restrictions limit the availability GMOs to certain countries.

The actual dangers that genetic modification could pose to the environment or, supposedly, individual health, are hotly contended.

Soil Conservation

In Dirt: The Erosion of Civilizations, geomorphologist David Montgomery outlines a coming crisis from soil erosion. Agriculture relies on roughly one meter of topsoil, and that is being depleted ten times faster than it is being replaced. No-till farming, which some claim depends upon pesticides, is regarded as one way to minimize erosion. However, a recent study by the USDA's Agricultural Research Service has found that manure applications in organic farming are better at building up the soil than no-till despite tillage.

Climate Change

In The Organic Answer to Climate Change, Anthony Meleca argues that organic agriculture - with its emphasis on closed nutrient cycles, biodiversity, and effective soil management - has the capacity to mitigate and even reverse the effects of climate change.

According to the Rodale Institute, which has been comparing organic agricultural systems and conventional systems since 1981, organic agriculture also can be used to mitigate global warming by decreasing fossil fuel emissions and sequestering carbon in the soil. The elimination of synthetic nitrogen in organic systems decreases fossil fuel consumption by 33 percent (LaSalle) and carbon sequestration takes CO2 out of the atmosphere by putting it in the soil in the form of organic matter which is often lost in conventionally managed soils. Carbon sequestration occurs at especially high levels in organic no-till managed soil according to the Rodale Institute.

Organic agriculture can reduce the level of negative externalities from (conventional) agriculture. Whether this is seen as private or public benefits depends upon the initial specification of property rights. However, it is clear that agriculture has been undervalued and underestimated as a means to combat global climate change. Soil carbon data recorded by The Rodale Institute show that regenerative organic agricultural practices are among the most effective strategies for mitigating CO_2 emissions.

Nutrient Leaching

Excess nutrients in lakes, rivers, and groundwater can cause algal blooms, eutrophication, and subsequent dead zones. In addition, nitrates are harmful to aquatic organisms by themselves. The main contributor to this pollution is nitrate fertilizers whose use is expected to "double or almost triple by 2050". Researchers at the United States National Academy of Sciences found that organically fertilizing fields "significantly [reduces] harmful nitrate leaching" over conventionally fertilized fields: "annual nitrate leaching was 4.4-5.6 times higher in conventional plots than organic plots".

Scientists believe that the large dead zone in the Gulf of Mexico is caused in large part by agricultural pollution: a combination of fertilizer runoff and livestock manure runoff. A study by the United States Geological Survey (USGS) found that over half of the nitrogen released into the Gulf comes from agriculture. The economic cost of this for fishermen may be large, as they must travel far from the coast to find fish.

At the 2000 IFOAM Conference, researchers presented a study of nitrogen leaching into the Danube River. They found that nitrogen runoff was substantially lower among organic farms and suggested that the external cost could be internalized by charging 1 euro per kg of nitrogen released.

A 2005 study found a strong link between agricultural runoff and algae blooms in California.

BIODIVERSITY

A wide range of organisms benefit from organic farming, but it is unclear whether organic methods confer greater benefits than integrated agri-environmental conventional programs. Nearly all non-crop, naturally occurring species observed in comparative farm land practice studies show a preference in organic farming both by population and richness. Spanning all associated species, there is an average of 30% more on organic farms versus conventional farming methods. Birds, butterflies, soil microbes, beetles, earthworms, spiders, vegetation, and mammals are particularly affected. Organic crops use little or no herbicides and pesticides and thus biodiversity fitness and population density benefit. Many weed species attract beneficial insects that improve soil qualities and forage on weed pests. Soil-bound organisms often benefit because of increased bacteria populations due to natural fertilizer spread such as manure, while experiencing reduced intake of herbicides and pesticides commonly associated with conventional farming methods. Increased biodiversity, especially from soil microbes such as mycorhizzae, have been proposed as an explanation for the high yields experienced by some organic plots, especially in light of the differences seen in a 21-year comparison of organic and control fields.

The level of biodiversity that can be yielded from organic farming provides a natural capital to humans. Species found in most organic farms provides a means of agricultural sustainability by reducing amount of human input (e.g. fertilizers, pesticides). Farmers that produce with organic methods reduce risk of poor yields by promoting biodiversity. Common game birds such as the ring-necked pheasant and the northern bobwhite often reside in agriculture landscapes, and are a natural capital yielded from high demands of recreational hunting. Because bird species richness and population are typically higher on organic farm systems, promoting biodiversity can be seen as logical and economical.

Biological research on soil and soil organisms has proven beneficial to the system of organic farming. Varieties of bacteria and fungi break down chemicals, plant matter and animal waste into productive soil nutrients. In turn, the producer benefits by healthier yields and more arable soil for future crops. Furthermore, a 21-year study was conducted testing the effects of organic soil matter and its relationship to soil quality and yield. Controls included actively managed soil with varying levels of manure, compared to a plot with no manure input. After the study commenced, there was significantly lower yields on the control plot when compared to the fields with manure. The concluded reason was an increased soil microbe community in the manure fields, providing a healthier, more arable soil system.

Sales and Marketing

Organic farmers report that marketing and distribution are difficult obstacles. Most of organic sales are concentrated in developed nations. These products are what economists call credence goods in that they rely on uncertain certification. As food prices rise, organic products may experience a decrease in quantity demanded. A 2008 survey by WSL Strategic Retail found that interest in organic products had dropped since 2006, and that 42% of Americans polled don't trust organic produce. The Hartman Group reports that 69% of Americans claim to occasionally buy organic products, down from 73% in 2005. The Hartman Group says that people may be substituting local produce for organic produce.

In the United States, 75% of organic farms are smaller than 2.5 hectares and in California 2% of the farms account for over half of the sales (Lotter 2003:4). Groups of small farms join together in cooperatives such as Organic Valley, Inc. to market their goods more effectively.

Over the past twenty years, however, most of these cooperative distributors have merged or been bought out. Rural sociologist Philip H. Howard has researched the structure and transformation of the organic industry in the

United States. He claims that in 1982 there were 28 consumer cooperative distributors but as of 2007 there are only 3, and he has created a graphic displaying the consolidation. His research shows that most of these small cooperatives have been absorbed into large multinational corporations such as General Mills, Heinz, ConAgra, Kellogg, and assorted other brands. This consolidation has raised concerns among consumers and journalists of potential fraud and degradation in standards. Most of these large corporations sell their organic products through subsidiaries, allowing them to keep their names off the labels.

Price premiums are important for the profitability of small organic farmers, and so many sell directly to consumers in farmers' markets. In the United States the number of farmers' markets has tripled from 1,755 in 1994 to 5,274 in 2009.

Organic agriculture can contribute to meaningful socio-economic and ecologically sustainable development, especially in poorer countries. On one hand, this is due to the application of organic principles, which means efficient management of local resources (e.g. local seed varieties, manure, etc.) and therefore cost-effectiveness. On the other hand, the market for organic products - at local and international level - has tremendous growth prospects and offers creative producers and exporters in the South excellent opportunities to improve their income and living conditions.

Organic Agriculture is a very knowledge intensive production system. Therefore capacity building efforts play a central role in this regard. There are many efforts all around the world regarding the development of training material and the organization of training courses related to Organic Agriculture. Big parts of existing knowledge is still scattered and not easily accessible. Especially in Developing Countries this situation remains an important constraint for the growth of the organic sector.

For that reason, the International Federation of Organic Agriculture Movements created an Internet Training Platform whose objective is to become the global reference point for Organic Agriculture training through free access to high quality training materials and training programs on Organic Agriculture. In November 2007, the Training Platform hosted more than 170 free manuals and 75 training opportunities.

A number of critics contest the notion that organic agricultural systems are more friendly to the environment and more sustainable than high-yielding farming systems. Among these critics are Norman Borlaug, father of the "green revolution", Nobel Peace Prize laureate, who asserts that organic farming practices can at most feed 4 billion people, after expanding cropland dramatically and destroying ecosystems in the process, and Prof A. Trewavas.

The debate has been summarized in an exchange between Trewavas and Lord P. Melchett, and published by a major supermarket, concerned about examining the issues.

A study from the Danish Environmental Protection Agency assessed the overall consequences of phasing out the total or partial use of pesticides. They looked at farming, market gardening, fruit growing, and forestry, and the effects of pesticides on health and the environment. It was estimated that phasing out all pesticides would result in an overall reduction of yield of about 25%. Environmental and health effects were assumed but hard to access, studies were recommended. In their conclusion they said, " The Committee recommends a reduction of the use of pesticides. The Committee finds that the optimisation of pesticide use could facilitate a reduction of treatment frequency in the treated areas of agriculture...without significant operating and socioeconomic losses."

In 2008 a study from UN Environmental Programme concluded that organic methods greatly increase yields in Africa and a review of over two hundred crop comparisons argued that organic farming could produce enough food per capita to sustain the current human population; the difference in yields between organic and non-organic methods were small, with non-organic methods resulting in slightly higher yields in developed areas and organic methods resulting in slightly higher yields in developing areas.

That analysis has been severely criticised by Alex Avery, who contends that the review claimed many non-organic studies to be organic, misreported organic yields, made false comparisons between yields of organic and non-organic studies which were not comparable, counted high organic yields several times by citing different papers which referenced the same data, and gave equal weight to studies from sources which were not impartial and rigorous university studies.

Urs Niggli, director of the FiBL Institute contends that the wave of newspaper articles like 'Organic food exposed' or 'The hypocrisy of organic farmers' are a part of a global campaign against organic farming that take their arguments mostly from the book 'The truth about organic farming', by Alex Avery of the Hudson Institute.

In 1998, Dennis Avery of the Hudson Institute claimed the risk of E. coli infection was eight times higher when eating organic food rather than non-organic food, using the Center for Disease Control (CDC) as a source. When the CDC was contacted, it stated that there was no evidence for the claim.

The New York Times commented on Avery's attacks: "The attack on organic food by a well-financed research organization suggests that, though organic food accounts for only 1 percent of food sales in the United States, the conventional food industry is worried."

Chapter 6

Cuisines in Beaches of Goa

Goa has multitude of restaurants spread across all over Goa. Varied Indian cuisine from the simple Goan fish curry and rice to rich Punjabi, tasty Manglorean, unlimited Gujarati Thalis & the most popular Udipi style food is available. The evergreen roadside "gadas" (carts) serving panipuri, bhel, pauvbhaji, omlette pauv, puri-bhaji and sugarcance juice are abundant.

Goa is an endearing destination of holiday makers in India. It is an important stop for foreign tourists visiting India. The real charm of Goa lies in its beaches that is a mix bag of serene beauty, excellent Goan cuisines and swaying palm trees. Goa beaches are an abode of sensuality and adventure. Of 125 km of marvelous coastline, the Goa sand beaches cover about 83 km. The exclusive tour packages to Goa facilitate the exploration of the popular beaches along with comfortable stay at the Goa beach resorts. The beaches in Goa therefore are thronged by honeymooners and adventure tourists every year. Salvage the popular gourmets and enjoy the warm waters, make your stay in Goa beaches memorable.

Delicious international cuisine is also a hallmark in Goa especially seen in scores of Chinese restaurants. Besides Chinese, you will find, German, Thai, Continental, Mexican, Lebanese, Italian and Health food restaurants.

Goa being a very liberal state, most of the restaurants serve alcohol freely.

We give below some of the popular restaurants in each category, where food & service is supposed to be of excellent quality and they are all worth visiting time and again.

GOAN FOOD - NORTH GOA

Souza' Lobo - Calangute Beach.

In existence for the past 65 years, this restaurant has earned its reputation on good food, good service & location. However, lately its been reported to have lost its quality of food. Still it's worth visiting at least once during your stay.

Mirabai's Goan Village - Calangute/Baga Road

Opened just about four months ago, this restaurant claims to offer only genuine goan food. Located on the main road, it has a simple ambience and is known to be quite popular. Food is supposed to be reasonably good but the service lacks in quality.

Sparrows Nest - Calangute Main Road

Located right besides the only Petrol Station in Calangute, this simple restaurant serves a mean Goan fish curry and rice dish, very popular with the locals and the tourists. Its prices are also very reasonable compared to others in the vicinity.

St. Anthony's Bar & Restaurant - Baga Beach

One of the oldest restaurants, it has a simple shack like ambience and some good food with friendly staff. Quite popular with tourists and well worth a visit.

Pagoda Chinese Restaurant

Situated on Baga Road, this is a neat place. Good Food and good service, but a bit steep on the prices.

Kim Fa Chinese Restaurant

On the Baga Road, next to Ronnil's Resort, this is quite a popular Chinese joint with good food at the right price. Quite popular with a lot of tourists and the owner Michael is a charmer.

China Highway

On the Calangute/Panaji Highway, this so called restaurant is situated in the fields and serves decent Chinese food at the right price. If you like outdoors, this is the place for you.

Palolem Beach

Among the beaches of Goa- Palolem Beach has the distinction of being the most stunning of the Goa beaches. The beach is adorned with extensive hut accommodation system and is rightly called the "Paradise Beach". The beach has been contributing to the tourism infrastructure in Goa in terms of the accommodation facilities and restaurants on the beach. Enjoy water sports like the bike tours, boat cruises and diving; great wine and local fenny in its restaurants that also specializes in sea food and Goan cuisines. Also drop into the dolphin spots. A vibrant night life adds to the charm of the place.

Palolem Beach resorts like the Alessandra resort, Brendon and the various beach huts are excellent places to put up while in Palolem.

Palolem Beach- Access: The Palolem Beach is located about 70 km from Panajim in Canacona of South Goa. The Goa International airport is a one hour drive and the nearest railway station is Canacona.

Mabor Beach

Goa India Mabor Beach is located south of Colva Beach and the Cavelossim beach. The place particularly boasts of luxury resorts and vibrant night life. Specialties of the Mabor Beach in Goa include the fishing village and the lagoon. Adventure tourists find the place a hot spot of activities like biking, parasailing and bump rides. The beach remained isolated until the 1980s. The Leela Beach Resort and other luxury hotel chains made the Mabor Beach popular among tourists.

Mabor Beach- Access: Dabolim is the nearest airport to the place that is 68 km from Mabor. The closest railway station is Karmali. You can also travel to Colva and then to Mabor by hiring a taxi.

Varca-Cavelossium Beach

The Varca Beach Goa has made its name in among the popular beach destinations for tourists in Goa. The Varca Beach also called the Cavelossium Beach gives a glimpse of the traditional fishing villages in Goa. Thatched roof houses and wooden shacks adorn the place. Historically it is inhabited by the Christian fishing folks of Goa. Prominent resorts in the Varca Beach are the Club Mahindra Varca Beach Resort, colonio Jose Menino and the Ramada Caravela Beach Resort. You can opt for lodging at the family houses as well.

Varca Beach- Access: The beach is 2 km of the Benaulim Beach down South Goa. The place is easily accessible from Margoa which is just 18 km from Varca. Dabolim airport is taxi drive of 47 km.

Colva - Benaulim Beach

Colva - also called the Colva- Benaulim Beach is one of the finest Goa beaches. The place is ideal for honeymooners who can enjoy the serene beauty and quietness of Goa by spending memorable moments in the Colva Beach in Goa. There are a variety of restaurants to choose from. They offer quality Goan and international food and drinks. The white sand beach of colva runs 20 km southwards of Goa. The other attraction of this place includes the Our Lady of Mercy Church famous for the annual fest Fama, celebrated since the 17th century. Christmas brings a new look to this beach every year.

Colva Beach- Access: The Colva- Benaulim beach in Goa is located around 40 km from Panaji and 2 km from the mouth of the Benaulim beach.

Dona Paula Beach

Dona Paula Beach Goa vacation could be an exotic experience with water sports bringing an additional thrill to the beauty of the place. The place is also a popular destination for shopping Goa handicrafts and dresses. Tourists indulge in sunbath, cruises and biking. Several traditional stories and myths attached to this place also lure tourists. You can find cheap and affordable accommodation in the Goa Dona Paula Beach and wooden eateries and liquor shops all around the place.

Dona Paula Beach- Access: The beach is 29 km from the Dabolim Airport. There is a ferry service from Marmagoa. You can also avail buses plying from Panjim's Kadamba bus stop.

Aguada Beach

The Aguada Beach in Goa is also known as the Fort Aguada Beach that is dominated by a large hill in the south of the beach. If you are looking out for solitude and peace, this is the best among all Goa beaches that you can opt. So what is special in the lonely Aguada Beach that makes it so interesting There are no restaurants lined up, no shopping hassles and no night life extravaganza. Quietness and loom rules this place. Relish few sweet moments with your loved one.

Aguada Beach- Access: Located in north Goa, the Aguada Beach is 4 km from the Sinquerim Beach. The place is an easy access from Fort Aguada.

Calangute Beach

Calangute Beach attractions are specially meant for the hippies, who discovered the place. European tourists throng the place especially during Christmas eve in Goa. Well known as the queen of the Goa beaches, the exquisite beauty of the place has been the major draw. The lined palm trees and the golden sand touching your feet; the Goa Calangute Beach is complete experience. Prominent attractions of this place includes the St Alex church and the Kerkar Art Complex. Water and sand sports activities and night cruises make this place interesting.

Calangute Beach- Access: Located on the shores of the Arabian Sea in north Goa, Calangute is 15 km from Panajim and easily accessible from Saligao and Candolim.

Baga Beach

The Baga Beach is an extension of the Calangute Beach in Goa. The beach merges along the Vagator Beach and Chapora beach coastline. A retreat house on the adjoining hill top adds to the grandeur of the Baga Beach. This beach has earned a name among the tourists for being a place of great food, wine and entertainment. British tourists have made the place particularly livelier. Night club of Tito's is famous for housing the only dance floor in Goa pubs.

Baga Beach- Access: Situated in the west coast of Goa and 10 km west of Mapusa, it is about 18 km from Panajim, the capital of Goa.

Miramar Beach

Miramir Beach Goa is also termed as Gasper Dias, and in Portuguese means "viewing the sea". This reference has made the serene Miramar Beach an important tourist place. Have a clear view of the Aguada Fort, and enjoy the chirping of about 500 species of migratory bird. Birdwatchers and researchers find the beach rejuvenating. Winter is the best season to visit the Miramar Beach to enjoy the migratory birds. A 15-minute walk through the sands would take you to riverfront venue of Dayanand Dandodker Marg.

Miramir Beach- Access: The beach is located in close proximity with the Panjim town. It is 29 km from the Dabolim. There are regular bus services from the Daula Paula beach which is just a km away.

Multicuisine & Speciality Restaurants

Oceanic

Right in Calangute Market Place, Oceanic is a multicuisine restaurant. Good food, good ambience its clientele is mostly regulars who visit them time and again.

Redonda

Located on the junction of Calangute/Baga Road, this restaurant is quite popular with tourists because of its location. A good place to sit out and while away your time looking around. Popular for Breakfasts.

Infantaria

In Calangute near the football field, this is a popular fast food restaurant for quick eat outs and breakfasts. It is however known to serve good snacks, and meals too.

Britto's

This popular restaurant is located right near the beach in Baga. Good Food and reasonable prices makes it quite popular with the locals as well as the tourists.

Fiesta

A great ambience with beautiful settings, this restaurant situated opposite Tito's Night Club in Baga, serves good Mediterranean and Italian cuisine.

Little Italy

Fighting for the same name, are two restaurants situated at different locations. Both claim to good genuine Italian food and both worth visiting. One is on the Calangute/Candolim road and the other one is in Little Baga opposite the river.

Plantain Leaf

Situated in the market place at Calangute this is a sprawling Vegetarian Restaurant, serving all kinds of Udipi style and now North Indian dishes. Reasonable food but sloppy service.

Udipi Restaurant

Just opposite the temple in Calangute, near Bank of Baroda, is this Indian vegetarian restaurant. Serves good udipi style south Indian food, but being small it is too crowded for some.

Palms N Sands

This restaurant is in Candolim, right on the beach with a 3 tier sit out. Serves good seafood and has great outdoor view of the sea.

Village Siesta

Unmatched ambience, quality food and personalized service is the trade mark of this restaurant situated in Siquerim. Serves multicuisine food.

Agonda Beach

The Agonda Beach huts are the noted feature that makes stay at the Agonda Beach both special and exciting. There are only two Goa beaches that provide this opportunity to travelers. Goa Agonda Beach is a 3 km lush of green cottages, cover 120 acres of forest land. Climb up the near by hill to the Cabo De Rama Fort that stands in ruins and have a spectacular sea view. The Agonda village beach boasts of hospitality and affordable accommodation to spend a long vacation amidst history and nature.

Agonda Beach- Access: You can hire a taxi from the Margao railway Station and the airport. It is an easy drop from the near by Palalem Beach Goa.

Majorda Beach

Goa beaches earn new appreciation with every visit to the Majorda Beach. It is an interesting place for the historical blend and the delicious breads. Majorda village is significant for the Goan toddy that was discovered in its limit. The art of baking European breads were first adopted by the Majorda locals. They hold the distinction of being the best bakers till date. As you drop into the Majorda Beach a traditional fervor is sure to wrap you. You would certainly take home the best breads in the country. If you are looking out for cheap stay and package search for homes in Majorda that is given on rent to tourists.

Majorda Beach- Access: You need to travel down south from Bogmalo. The Mahorda Beach Resort can be reached from Colva Beach that is at a distance of 8 km.

Vagator Beach

Of the northern most beaches in Goa, the Vagator Beach is one of the major haunts of the foreigners. The beach is beauty personified with red cliffs and fresh water springs located near by. The beach is divided in two sections namely the Big Vagator Beach and Little Vagator Beach. You can experience the best night life jazz on this beach at the Nine Bar, located hilltop and the Primrose discotheque that has renowned DJ's.

The Mediterranean food and drink bars have a large tourists traffic of both Indian and foreign visitors.

Vagator Beach- Access: Dabolim is the nearest airport located approximately 22 km from the beach. It is 24 km from Panaji. Karmali is the nearest railway point.

Bagmalo Beach

As the Bagmalo is a small serene village in Goa, the Bagmalo Beach is an enticing experience for those Goa travelers who prefer enjoying the warm waters than go for any wild adventure or great delicacies. Traditionally a fishing village, the Bagmalo Beach in Goa offers visitors with perfect blend of attraction places and village lifestyle. Several foreigners have also purchased vacation homes and guest houses along the Bagmalo Beach. The presence of the Oberoi Hotel also makes it a sought after place.

Bagmalo Beach- Access: Airport is 18 km from Dabolim Airport and 8 km from Panaji.

Anjuna Beach

Luxury beach resorts and gambling centers along the Anjuna Beach is a significant draw to foreign tourists compared to other Goa beaches. It is dubbed as the hippie capital of Goa. Hard rocks border the Goa Anjuna Beach. Tap your feet as you remember the tunes of "Anjunabeats"- signature level for Above & Beyond music group. Exploring Anjuna beach would be celebrating life amidst beauty and wild music, parties and shopping. Historical attractions of the place include Chapora Fort, Albuquerque mansion and its octagonal towers.

Anjuna Beach- Access: It is located 18 km from the capital city of Panajim. Buses plying from Mapusa drop passengers along the Tarmac road across the Anjuna village.

Goan Food - Panaji

Mum's Kitchen

Situated on the road to Miramar in Panaji, this restaurant is quite famous with the local residents and tourists alike for its good Goan food.

Jasima

Located near the 'Junta House' just off the 18th June road. The food is decent and is reasonably priced. Service during lunchtime is lousy because the management and staff are busy watching the TV.

Vegetarian Restaurants

Hotel Kamat

Located on the church square in Panaji, this popular restaurant serves vegetarian food in Udipi style.

Satkar Hotel

Situated on 18th June Road in Panaji, this is another Udipi style restaurant serving the standard South Indian dishes.

Multicuisine & North Indian Restaurants

Delhi Darbar

Ask anybody and they will guide you to this most popular restaurant. Nice ambience, good Tandoori and

North Indian food. The prices are a bit steep for Indian Standards.

Sher - e - Punjab

Another popular name in the North Indian food scene, they have two restaurants with the same name in Panaji and serves decent North Indian cuisine.

White House - Donna Paula

Situated on the Donna Paula hillock overlooking the Governor's Palace, it has an excellent view of both Panaji and Marmugoa harbour. The place is more for relaxing for an evening drink and some snacks, but as far as the food is concerned it is nothing special.

South Goa

Martins Nest - Betalbatim

Located close to the Betalbatim beach, this restaurant is known for its genuine goan food. A family run business, its service is good by goan standards. Best to visit during weekdays, as Saturdays & Sundays are awfully crowded.

Lounginohs - Margao

Situated in the heart of Margao city near to the Municipal Buildings, this restaurant has the ambience of a pub and serves excellent Goan, Chinese and continental dishes. Their cocktails are well recommended.

Coco Loco

At Agassaim, on the way between Panaji and Margao, this restaurant is situated in the midst of shady palm groove. Good for seafood and Goan food.

Kentuckee

On the Colva Beach in South Goa. This restaurant serves good seafood and also has a multicuisine menu. Open till late night, its sea front location is ideal for a night out with good food.

Zeebop Restaurant

Right on Utorda Beach, opposite Kenilworth Beach Resort. This outdoor restaurant has a great setting. While you wait for you food, you can relax on one of the cane chairs or a hammock sipping a cool drink. Serves exotic goan food.

Banjara

Located in Margao, this restaurant takes pride to call itself the finest Indian restaurant in Goa. Worth one visit if you are in Margao.

Fiplees Restaurant

On Benaulim beach, this restaurant is a one-stop hot spot serving multicuisine meals. They also conduct a lot of theme parties and Buffet Dinner.

Arambol Beach holidays are sheer delight as the beach takes you far away from the usual Goan life. The uniqueness of this place lies in the secluded and primitive look that it wears. People looking for tranquility find it a perfect destination in Goa. There are attractive bays and a fresh water lake north of the Arambol beach and rocky headlands separate the swimming pools. You may find good accommodation even in the areas surrounding the Arambol Beach Goa.

Arambol Beach- Access: You can avail bus services that ply from Mapusa and Chopdem to Arambol.

Chapter 7

Low Calories Food in High Altitude Hill Stations

The low calorie food list shows some great everyday foods which are low in calories and ideal for weight loss diets. The calorie content is shown in the foods average portion. The low calorie food list also gives calorie content in 100 grams so it can be compared with other foods you may normally eat.

We want the low calorie food list to grow larger so if you know of a good low calorie food for weight loss please let us know about it email us.

Apart from the low calorie food list below there are 5 other lists that show the calorie content of everyday foods use the links below to view these useful tables.

Low calorie food	Portion size	100 grams (3.5 oz)	energy content
Beans mung dried boiled	100 cals	100 cals	Low
Beans runner boiled	15 cals	25 cals	Very low
Broccoli	20 cals	30 cals	Very low
Brussels sprouts	20 cals	32 cals	Low
Canderel sweetener	10 cals / tablet	-	Low

Low calorie food	Portion size	100 grams (3.5 oz)	energy content
Cottage cheese low fat	80 cals	80 cals	Low
Fish any white fresh poached	150-200 / fillet	110 cals	Low
Fromage Frais low fat	65 cals	55 cals	Low-Med
Hunts bitter lemon drink	2 (125ml)	1 cal	Low-Med
Hunts bitter Ginger ale drink	2 (125ml)	1 cal	Low
Hunts bitter orange drink	2 (125ml)	1 cal	Low
Lentils	70 cals	50 cals	Low
Macaroni (boiled)	238 cals (250g)	95 cals	Low
Mayonnaise weight watchers	45 cals (1 Tbsp)	300 cals	Lowe
Muesli sugar-free	180 cals (50g)	360 cals	Low
Noodles (boiled)	175 cals (250g)	70 cals	Low
Pasta (normal boiled)	330 cals (300g)	110 cals	Low
Pasta (wholemeal boiled)	315 cals (300g)	105 cals	Low
Peas chick boiled	115 cals	115 cals	Low
Porridge oats (with water)	193 cals (350g)	55 cals	Low

Low calorie food	Portion size	100 grams (3.5 oz)	energy content
Potatoes (boiled)	210 cals (300g)	70 cals	Low
Rice (white long grain)	420 cals (300g)	140 cals	Low
Rice (Brown)	405 cals (300g)	135 cals	Low
Spaghetti (boiled)	303 cals (300g)	101 cals	Low
Tofu	90 cals	73 cals	Low
Yogurt virtually fat-free	50 cals (1 small pot)	40 cals	Low

Portion sizes will vary depending on the type and make of product purchased. Portion size is very often a subjective view and may again vary according to bowl, cup or plate size used.

NB. The low calorie food list shows products in alphabetical order.

Most natural foods are calculated in tests and specific product values are calculated from their ingredients list or from manufacturers information. Some values may not be accurate and should only be used for general comparison purposes.

This chapter gives you information about Shimla restaurants that are famous for serving varieties of delicious cuisines to their guests. Most of the Shimla restaurants are renowned for serving typical Himachali food that a tourist should opt for to tantalize their taste buds.

A favorite and most loved food item is 'Luchi-Poti' made with lamb intestines is a good item for non vegetarian food lovers. The 'Momos' of Shimla are another hot item served in restaurants.

Shimla ia a city, that is visited by numerous international tourists, so the restaurants in Shimla is said to offer a variety of mouth watering cuisines to its guests. The pasta in popular restaurants of Shimla is served with variety of sauces and delight the food eaters.

One can get a wide range of regional as well as international dishes prepared with perfection by some of the renowned chefs in the restaurants of Shimla.

Almost all the restaurants in Shimla are offer cheap and comfortable atmosphere with quality multi-cuisine food. But the menus of local cuisine are surprisingly limited. Here is a list of some of the renowned restaurants of Shimla.

" Seventh Heaven "

Hotel Combermere, The Mall,

Ph No:: 0177 251246 - 48 / 252242 / 252243 / 252246 / 252248

" The Lutyen'S Room

Springfields, Opposite Tibetan School,

Chotta Shimla

Ph No:: 0177 221297 / 221298

" Bhasoli Restaurant

Kufri Holiday Resort, Kufri Village, Kufri

Ph No:: 0177 480341 / 480342 / 480343

" Baljees Restaurant

26, The Mall,

Ph No:: 0177 258926 / 252313

" Silver Oak Restaurant

Circular Road, Shimla

Ph No:: 0177 257588 / 257589

" The Devicos Restaurant

5, The Mall Road,

Ph No:: 0177 206335 / 208261

" Cecil, Chaura Maidan,

Oberoi,

Ph No: 91 177 280-4848

People are so calorie conscious that before buying any foodstuff they check for ingredients and calories. Sedentary lifestyle makes you opt for low calorie diet menu. If you can lower your daily calorie intake by 500 calories, you will be able to lose one pound per week. Men and women, both like to flaunt when they have a fabulously contoured body, the right curves at the right places!

A low calorie diet allows you to shed unwanted fat and lose weight. Only cutting down the number of calories may lead to vitamins and nutrients deficiency which can result in serious health complications. To avoid this, you should opt for a low calorie weight loss diet menu which includes all the food types such as proteins, carbohydrates, fiber, good fats, etc. You may come across various low calorie diets like 1000, 1500 or 1600 calorie diet but you should opt for a balanced diet which is suitable for your lifestyle.

Weight loss can not be achieved by only lowering the number of calories from the daily calorie intake, you need to burn more calories than the calories consumed. The low calorie diet plan should not affect your body metabolism or should not lead to dysfunction of any of the body systems. Sudden weight loss can result in fatigue and can affect your working capacity. Cutting down too many calories suddenly can make you leave the diet halfway. Calorie intake can vary from person to person and it depends upon age, sex, physical activity, overall physical and mental health of the person. If you are thinking about how to plan a low calorie diet menu, then you should keep it in mind that only a healthy diet can keep you healthy. Low calorie diet menu for women and low calorie diet menu for men may vary, depending mainly upon the age, health and physical activity. You should set realistic and attainable diet goals. While on diet you should follow the following guidelines.

Guidelines for Following low calorie diet menu:

Rather than eating 2-3 meals, you should consume 4 - 6 small meals and snacks everyday.

You should always have fresh and low-fat foods around, and for that you should plan your menu well in advance.

Always try simple menus and don't get too caught up on specifics.

Avoid high calorie foods, foods rich in fat, sweets, desserts, candies, pastries, processed foods, junk or fast foods, etc.

You should opt for a high fiber diet as it maintains your digestive health.

All types of foods such as fresh fruits, vegetables, whole grains cereals, beans, low fat versions of dairy products and meat and poultry, fish, etc. should be included in daily low calorie diet menu.

Here is a sample healthy low calorie diet menu (1573 calories).

Darjeeling, the Queen of Hills, the beautiful hamlet nestled in the lap of mighty Himalayas and set against the ravishing view of the peak, Kanchenjunga, is a must-visit place in India. Darjeeling has a very interesting cuisine to offer. Food is never a problem in Darjeeling as it is populated by local eateries offering the typical Darjeeling delicacies and has very multi cuisine good restaurants. Being inhabited by numerous Tibetans and Nepalese, the local eateries as well as the restaurants in Darjeeling offer many dishes common to Nepalese and Tibetan cuisine like thupka, momo, churpee and wai wai. Churpees are delicious chewing gums made out of cow's milk or yak's milk. It is a local delicacy. Momos are soft melt-in-the-mouth dumplings stuffed with vegetables or meat. Normally they are served with steaming hot watery soups. Wai wai and thupkas is a sort of thick noodles served dry or in soup, but invariably piping hot. Eating in a local eatery, taking in the serenity of the surroundings, smelling the cool fragrant air is an absolutely wonderful experience that beckons one back to the place, over and over again. These local eateries are there in every nook and corner of this serene town.

Tea is generally the preferred drink in India. More so in Darjeeling with its expansive tea gardens and the finest quality of tea produced. Tongba is a local beer that is 100% alcohol free and is very popular among the tourists. Chhang is yet another local beer available, and is made out of millets. Dining out in one of the restaurants in Darjeeling is a pleasant experience, indeed. The restaurants in Darjeeling offer a wide array of food like hot, spicy and unbelievably flavoured Indian cuisine, Chinese food, Italian delicacies and Continental dishes. Their menu ranges from regional dishes to international cuisine. Many of them also serve the local delicacies, which constitutes mainly of the Nepalese and Tibetan delicacies. Some restaurants organise live music to entertain the guests.

Some of the popular joints in Darjeeling are Glenary Restaurant, Keventers Restaurant, Dekevas Restaurant and Mayfair Hotel. Glenary Restaurant is a multi-cuisine restaurant near Chowrasta. It also has a bakery adjoined to it. Keventers Restaurant is famous for its burgers, hotdogs and sauces, provided at reasonable prices. Dekevas is on the ground floor of Dekeling hotel and is famous for its mouth-watering Tibetan Cuisine. It is famous for its wonton soup, momos, Shabalay and tsampa roasted barley served with butter, cheese and milk. The restaurant of Mayfair Hotel is most popular for its sumptuous buffet of Indian food. It also offers the continental cuisine.

Another thing to enjoy in Darjeeling is an afternoon tea with tiffin. The tiffin along with the afternoon tea in Darjeeling consists of a variety of cakes. Darjeeling tea is a mild brew, compared to strongly flavoured tea preferred in India.

Altogether, eating out in Darjeeling can be an experience varied by the eateries or restaurants the traveller prefers. The popular restaurants in Darjeeling provide good ambience as well as delectable food. The atmosphere in bustling local eateries, serving the Nepalese and Tibetan delicacies, is also a different experience. Actually, in Darjeeling, the tourist may be spoilt for choices. The Tibetan and Nepalese cuisine is a must-try in Darjeeling.

Its very normal that a hot tourist destination like Ooty will have some decent restaurants and eateries. However more than that, the presence of several outstanding Restaurants in Ooty have made the city a food freak's paradise.

Some of the most frequented cafes, bars and Restaurants in Ooty are mentioned below:

- Blue hills
- Chandan Vihar
- Chinkos Chinese Restaurant
- Hills Palace
- Tandoor Mahal
- Ooty Coffee House

Most of the hotels and resorts in the lovely hill station of Ooty have first class multi cuisine restaurants within their complexes. Some of the hotels with restaurants are:

- Sterling Holiday Resorts
- Hotel PNR
- Hotel Preethi Palace
- Hotel Royal Paradise
- Hotel Saffire Paradise
- Hotel Tripless
- Hotel Savoy Sylks
- Hotel Southern Star
- Hotel Sri Ganapathy
- Hotel Sweekar
- Hotel Tamilnadu Tourism
- Hotel Tamilnadu

These Ooty restaurants serve authentic dishes of south Indian, north India, Chinese, Continental, Thai, Mexican,

Bengali and other cuisines. Few hotel cum restaurants in Ooty is open throughout the day while many of them have dawn to dusk services. The bar cum restaurants of the town serves all types of branded wines and mouth watering snacks and dishes. A food lover in Ooty will live in cloud nine, binging on those lip smacking culinary delights.

The popularity of Mussoorie ensures that a wide range of quick eats and cuisines are available here. The pleasant hill weather and climb builds a good appetite. Numerous cafes, including Barista and Café Coffee Day, along the Mall offer a picturesque setting for evening chats and hot food.

One of the most popular hill stations in India, Mussoorie isn't known as the Queen of the Hills for nothing. Located in the foothills of the Himalayas, Mussoorie offers the breathtaking spectacle of the majestic snow-capped mountains in the northeast, as well as panoramic views of the Doon Valley and the beautiful city of Dehradun. Barely an hour's drive from Dehradun, the last rail-head, and five hours' drive from Delhi by road, Missoorie is easily accessible by rail or by road and makes the perfect getaway for leisure and weekend tourists. While hotels in Mussoorie are a dime a dozen, only a few make the cut as the hill station's best. Whether it's luxurious comfort or warm hospitality, these five-star hotels have the very best to offer.

Jaypee Residency Manor

Located on a beautiful hill top and spread over nine acres of lush greenery, Jaypee Residency Manor's well appointed rooms offer stunning views of the majestic Himalayas. One of the finest five-star hotels in Mussoorie, it features all modern amenities, including an indoor heated swimming pool, fitness center, jogging track, spa with sauna and steam, bowling alley, skating rink, pool tables and children's library. The lounge, cafe and multi-cuisine restaurant serve the finest in Indian and continental cuisines and offer a selection of the best wine and liquors.

Fortune Resort Grace

Offering a beautiful view of the Doon valley, the Fortune Resort Grace is spread over 32 acres on a pine-covered hill slope. Done up in contemporary decor, all the 74 rooms come equipped with modern amenities like high speed Internet access, 32-inch LCD televisions and electronic safes. The beautiful five-star resort also features a business center, banquet hall, foreign currency exchange, babysitting facilities, gymnasium and a recreational center with pool tables and a kids' play zone. Multi-cuisine restaurants and a contemporary lounge offer an array of fine cuisines and a selection of the finest wines and spirits.

Claridges Nabha Residence

Once the summer residence of the erstwhile Maharaja of Nabha, The Claridges Nabha Residence is surrounded by 13.5 acres of cedar forests and perched on a lush green hill top. With its wide, wrap-around verandas and distinctly Victorian architecture reminiscent of the colonial era, this five-star hotel offers 22 deluxe or duplex rooms, each with a breathtaking view of the cedar forest. Wireless Internet connection, television with satellite channels, DVD player and attentive room service ensure optimum comfort for the leisure tourist, while the large board rooms with all modern amenities are sure to be a big draw for the business traveler. The hotel features an all-day restaurant serving an array of Indian and continental cuisines, a well-stocked bar, and an impressive library for those who want to cuddle up with a good book.

The Claridges Nabha Residence

Airfield, Barlowgunj

Mussoorie, Uttarakhand, India 248 179

+91 135 2631 426, +91 135 2631 427

claridges-hotels.com

Mussoorie Hotels

Hotel Honeymoon Inn, Mussoorie

Comfort hotel and luxury resort in Mussoorie with 59 rooms, library, discotheque, conference facility, travel counter, laundry, billiards, table tennis and restaurant services.

Address: The Mall, Mussoorie - 248 179, India

Web: http://www.hotelhoneymooninn.net/mussoorie/

Hotel Gracemount

Hotel in Mussoorie having 70 well appointed rooms & suites, lush green estate, terrace restaurant, multi cuisine restaurant cum coffee shop, conference hall, grand lobby, multi utility hall, indoor water fall for kids and car parking area.

Address: Library Chowk, Mussoorie - 248 179, India

Sterling Holiday Resorts (I) Ltd., Mussoorie

Banquet and Conference facilities, Shopping Arcade, Games Room. 45 kms. from Dehradun Airport. 35 kms. from Dehradun Railway Station. Room Service, H/C running water, Telephone, T.V., Channel Music, Fully equipped kitchennete.

Address: Radha Bhavan Estate, Circular Road, Mussoorie - 248 179, India.

Hotel White House

Providing room services with hot and cold water and cable t.v..

Address: Near J. P. Hotel, Barlowgunj, Mussoorie - 248 179, India

Hotel Nand Residency

Providing 3 star hotel services.

Address: Nandvilla Estate, The Mall Kulri, Mussoorie - 248 179, India

Hotel Green Castle

Deluxe hotel in Mussoorie with super deluxe rooms having modern facilities like 24 hour running hot and cold water, conference hall, multicuisine restuarant, discotheque, health club and also offering special honeymoon package.

Address: The Mall, Mussoorie - 248 179, India

Hotel Deep

Provides services for 39 DB rooms with all modern amenities

Address: Camel Back Road, Kulri, Mussoorie - 248 179, India

Dunsvirk Court

Banquet Facilities, Corom, Chess, Badminton, Billiards. Room Service, H/C running water, Telephone, C.C.T.V.. 1km. from Bus Stand. 40 kms. from Airport. 36 kms from Railway Station.

Address: Baroda Estate, Library, Mussoorie - 248 003, India

Hotel Padmini Nivas

5 minutes walk from Library bus stand & Main Market. Children;s Play Ground, Yoga, Table Tennis, Indoor games. 60 kms from Airport. 35 kms from Railway Station.

Address: The Mall, Library, Mussoorie - 248 179, India

Kasmanda Palace Hotel

Providing hotel services with all facilities.

Address: The Mall Road, Mussoorie - 248 179, India

Roselynn Estate Hotel

Hotel with 42 rooms close to downtown area providing Indian, chinese, tandoori cuisines. Other facilities include conference hall , safe deposit lockers, car rental etc.

Address: The Mall, Mussoorie - 248 179, India

Hotel Connaught Castle

Heart of the Town. Banquet & Conference Facilities. Room Service, H/C running water, Telephone, Fax, T.V., Channel Music. Doctor on Call, Laundry, Travel Desk Service. 3 kms. from Bus Stand. 48 kms from Airport. 35 kms from Railway Station.

Address: Kulri, The Mall, Mussoorie - 248 179, India

Hotel Filigree

Govt. approved hotel , with facilities of cable TV, heating arrangements, electronic exchange (EPABX) etc.

Address: Camel's back Road , Kulri, Mussoorie - 248 179, India

Fortune Dunsvirk Court

Govt. approved hotel , with 43 rooms serving mughlai , indian, chinese, continental cuisines , credit cards accepted.

Address: Dunsvirk Court, Baroda Estate Library, Mussoorie - 248 179, India

Hotel Charlene

Hotel with good hospitable services

Address: Kulri, The Mall, Mussoorie, India

Hotel Shiva Continental

Govt. approved 2 star hotel, centrally heated, multicuisines, credit cards accepted, offer most reasonable rates with special packages for off season and groups.

Address: Near Picture Palace, The Mall, Kulri, Mussoorie - 248 179, India

Hotel Brentwood

Situated towards the kulri end of the mall, is one of the best hotel's in town.The hotel with 64 rooms and suites provides all modern facilities like,cctv,ampleparking,restaurant, doctor on call, pool, health club etc.

Address: Kulri, Mussoorie - 248 179, India

Hotel Classic Heights

Hotel with good hospitable services accepting credit cards also

Address: Library Chowk, Mussoorie - 248 179, India

Hotel The Pearl - A Royal Residency

Hotel located on the beautiful hills, provides multi cuisines . Other facilities include conference room, central fresh unit , elevator etc.

Address: Kalsia Estate, Opp. Picture Palace, Kulri, Mussoorie - 248 169, India

Savoy Hotel, Mussoorie

Business Centre, Executive Lounge, Banquet Facilities, Two Conference Halls, Ball Room with Nightly dancing with Band and Cabaret (in season), Dry Cleaning, Tennis, Squash, Billiards, Hiking, Fishing, Trekking, Horse Back Riding and Sight Seeing.

Address: The Mall, Mussoorie - 248 179, India

Hotel Midtown, Mussoorie

Hotel with Indian, chinese,continental cuisines . Facilities for conference hall, cable TV, good room service

Address: The mall, Mussoorie - 248 179, India

Hamers International

Hotel with Indian, chinese, continental cuisines. Facilities for conference hall, furnished rooms with CCTV , revolving restaurant, money exchange etc.

Address: The Mall, Mussoorie - 248 179, India

VALLEY VIEW HOTEL

Situated on the Mall road & Close to Rolley Car. 50 kms from Airport. 36 km from Railway Station.

Address: The Mall Kulri, Mussoorie - 248 179, India

HOTEL DOON PLACE

Hotel with all modern facilities and comforts .

Address: Kulri Bazar, Mussoorie - 248 179, India

HOTEL ABHINANDAN

Hotel with a beautiful panaromic view of sun kissing Shivalik peaks . Also available are other hospitality services.

Address: The mall, Kurli, Mussoorie - 248 179, India

COUNTRY INN, MUSSOORIE

Hotel with good hospitable services , transport arrangements, recreation facilities , creit cards accepted

Address: Kincretg, Haya Colie Estate, Nalapani House, Mussoorie - 248 179, India

COUNTRY INN MUSSORIE

Partially Air-conditioned. Hill Resort. Banquet Facilities, Indoor Games. Room Service, H/C running water, Telephone, Fax, T.V.. Doctor on Call, Laundry. 300 km from Airport. 26 km from Railway Station. 26 Km from Dehradun.

Address: Kincreig - Distt Dehradun, Mussoorie - 248 179, India

JAYPEE RESIDENCY MANOR

5 Star Deluxe Hotel. Centrally Heated. 4 kms from Mall, spreadover 09 acres of Hilly Terrain, 360 degree Panoramic View of Hill. Beauty Parlour, Shopping Arcade, Health Club, Swimming Pool, Tennis, Golf, Discotheque, Water Sports. 55 kms from Airport.

Address: Bar Lowganj, Mussoorie - 248 122, India

Hotel Ashoka Continental

One minutre walk from Library, Gandhi Chowk, Bus & Taxi stands.. Yoga, Trekking, Sight seeings. 60 kms. from Airport. 34 kms. from Railway Station.

Address: Library, The Mall, Mussoorie - 248 179, India

Hotel Kasmanda Lodge

Hotel with Indian, tandoori, continental cuisines. Arrangement for guided tours to historic and beautiful places , adventure safari , car services etc.

Address: The Mall, Mussoorie - 248 179, India

Hotel Western

On the Main Mall Road. Room Service, A/C running water, Telephone, T.V., Channel Music. 30 kms from Railway Station.

Address: The Mall, Mussoorie - 248 179, India

Shipra Hotel, Mussoorie

Centrally Located Near Bus Stand. Banquet & Conference Facilities, Shopping Arcade. Room Service, H/C running water, Telephone, Fax, T.V., Safe Deposit, Channel Music, Tea/Coffee maker. Doctor on Call, Laundry, Safe Deposit. 0.5 kms. from Bus Stand.

Address: Picture Palace, The Mall Picture Palace, The Mall, Mussoorie - 248 179, India

Hotel Shivam, Mussoorie

Hotel on the hills with facilities for tour and travel, car rental, doctor on call, safe deposit lockers etc.

Address: Opp. Picture Palace, Mussoorie - 248 179, India

Amar Hotel

Available best rooms in heart of the town for budget tourists, special discount to groups, students,Rotarians, Masons all round the year.

Address: New Market,Kulri,The Mall, Mussoorie - 248 179, India

Hotel Samrat, Mussoorie

Hotel with all modern facilitiies . Exclusive car parking , CCTV , Indian and continental cuisines.

Address: The Mall, Mussoorie - 248 179, India

Hotel Howard International

Hotel with Indian, chinese, continental cuisines. Facilities for conference hall, furnished rooms with CCTV , revolving restaurant, money exchange etc.

Address: The Mall, Mussoorie - 248 179, India

Shilton Hotel, Mussoorie

Main Mall Road. H/C running water, telephones, CTV, cable connection.. Library bus stand. 55 kms from airport. 32 Kms from railway station.

Address: Library Bazar, Mussoorie - 248 179, India

Hotel Apsara, Mussorie

Hotel with all modern facilities and amenities

Address: Opp. Picture Palace , The mall, Mussoorie - 248 179, India

Hotel Mitsons Private Limited

Hotel with Indian cuisines , good management and accepts credit cards

Address: Near Masonic Lodge Bus Stand, Kulri, Mussoorie - 248 179, India

Valallah Hotels (P) Ltd.

Hotel located besides the trolley car , rooms with kitchen , coffee shop etc.

Address: The Mall, Mussoorie - 248 179, India

Avalon Resorts

Located on slopes of Gunhill, Highest point in Mussoorie with fully furnished independent cottages with latest amenities.. Games Room, Conference Room, Gymnaesium, Multi-Cuisine Restaurant, Snack Bar, In house departmental store. 55 kms. from Airport.

Address: Gunhill, Mussoorie - 248 179, India

Hotel Piknik

Hotel with all modern facilities and amenities.

Address: Opp. Picture Palace , The Mall, Mussoorie - 248 169, India

Hotel Shining Star

Hotel with multi cuisines . Facilities for room heating system , safe deposit , accepts credit cards etc.

Address: The Mall , Library Opp. Vasu Theatre, Mussoorie - 248 179, India

Claridges Nabha Resort

Hotel with good hospitable services, accepts credit cards

Address: Barlowganj Road, Mussoorie - 248 179, India

Ambica Resorts Private Limited

Luxurious hotel with suites and honemooning rooms , good management and services

Address: The Mall, Library, Mussoorie - 248 179, India

Hotel Solitaire Plaza

Govt. approved 3 star hotel , with Indian, chinesc, continental cuisines. Facilities of conference hall, credit cards etc.

Address: Picture Palace , Kinrag Road, Mussoorie - 248 179, India

Hotel Horizon, Mussoorie

Next to the kulri shopping centre of Mussoorie. Doctor on Call, Laundry, Travel Desk Service. 100 yds. from Masonic Lodge Bus Stand. 60 kms. from Airport. 35 kms. from Railway Station.

Address: Kulri The Mall, Mussoorie - 248 179, India

Residency Manor

Govt. approved hotel . Banquet facilities , centrally heated and centrally airconditioned, swimmig pool, accepts credit cards etc,

Address: Barlowganj, Mussoorie - 248 122, India

There are many restaurants in Mussoorie which are ideal place for dining. Some of the eating out restaurants in Mussoorie, other than your regular hotel meals are as follows:

The Green Mall

This place is known to serve an amazing biryani from locally grown basmati rice and makes it a treat to dine here. People give priority to kurli's biryani than Chinese food.

JP's Residency Manor

It is the only five star hotel in Mussorie, Barlowganj and it offers variety of cuisines and wines.

Omi Sweet Shop

It is a renowned Century Old Sweet Shop in Landour Bazaar serving delicious sweets and other products since 1860.

Rice Bowl

It is the best place to eat for Chinese and Tibetan food in Mussoorie. Run by a very friendly Tibetan family the food offered by them is delicious and cheap as well.

Bibliography

- Tourism, Promotion And Power: Creating Images, Creating Identities by N. J. Morgan, Annette Pritchard, ISBN: 0471983411, ISBN-13: 9780471983415, 978-0471983415, Binding: Hardcover, Publishing Date: Jan 1999, Publisher: John Wiley & Sons, Edition: 1970th Edition, Number of Pages: 272, Language: English
- Customer Service and the Luxury Guest by Paul Ruffino.
- Fustel De Coulanges. The Ancient City: Religion, Laws, and Institutions of Greece and Rome.
- Bolchazy. Hospitality in Antiquity: Livy's Concept of Its Humanizing Force.
- Eric Larson, 2003 p135, The Devil in the White City; Murder, Magic, and Madness at the Fair that Changed America. Citing Chicago Tribune, Nov. 9, 1889.
- Aerial Extreme Sports (2008). History of Bungee.
- "Can you Hackett?" Unlimited - Inspiring Business. 23 August 2004.
- "AJ Hackett Bungy". Bungy.co.nz.
- "Guinness World Record - the Highest Commercial Decelerator Descent". Macautower.com.mo. 2005-08-17. http://www.macautower.com.mo/eng/press/award02.asp.
- CRUZ FILHO, F. Murillo, Bartolomeu Lourenço de Gusmão: Sua Obra e o Significado Fáustico de Sua Vida, Rio de Janeiro, Biblioteca Reprográfica Xerox, 1985

- SILVA, Inocencio da, ARANHA, Brito, Diccionario Bibliographico Portuguez, Lisboa, Imprensa Nacional, T. I, pp. 332-334.
- Asheim, G. 1999. Economic analysis of sustainability. In: W.M. Lafferty and O. Langhalle, Editors, Towards Sustainable Development, St. Martins Press, New York, p. 159
- Pezzey, J. 1989. Economic Analysis of Sustainable Growth and Sustainable Development, Environmental department Working Paper No. 15, World Bank.
- Barbier, E. 2007 Natural Resources and Economic Development, Cambridge University Press
- Jungmin Lee,(2004)Extreme Sports Evaluation: Evidence from Judging Figure Skating,Econometric Society
- Tomlinson, Joe (2004). Extreme Sports: In Search of the Ultimate Thrill. Hove: Firefly Books Ltd. ISBN 1-55297-992-X.
- "Ernest Hemingway FAQ part 5".
- "Extreme Sports - Encarta". Microsoft Encarta Online Encyclopedia. 2008. Archived from the original on 2009-10-31.
- "'Generation Y' Drives Increasingly Popular...". AmericanSportsData.com. August 1, 2002.
- Brymer, Eric and Gray, Tonia, Extreme Sports: A Challenge to Phenomenology. University of Wollongong, Australia, 2004
- Brymer, Eric, Extreme Dude: A Phenomenological Perspective on the Extreme sports experience . University of Wollongong, Australia, 2005
- Eadington, W.R., and V.L. Smith (1992). The emergence of alternative forms of tourism, in Tourism Alternatives: Potentials and Problems in the Development of Tourism. Pennsylvania, USA: University of Pennsylvania Press.
- Kim S.S. and A.M. Morrison, 'Change of Images of South Korea among Foreign Tourists after the 2002 FIFA World Cup', Tourism Management, 26, 2 (2005), 233–47.

Index